The
Knitter's
Year

The Knitter's Year

52 SIMPLE SEASONAL KNITS

DEBBIE BLISS

PHOTOGRAPHY BY PENNY WINCER

Quadrille
PUBLISHING

In memory of my wonderful mother, Mid.

When it comes to knitting, to my mind there is an immense amount of pleasure to be gained from picking up a project that can be easily completed in a short amount of time. With most of us contending with busy, if not frantic lifestyles, when we do manage to carve out a small oasis of calm, it is often all too brief. But these short spells of downtime can be the perfect moments to craft something that demands very little from us apart from a pair of needles, a small quantity of yarn and an equal amount of enthusiasm.

With this in mind, I have created *The Knitter's Year*. This book offers 52 designs to take you all the way from spring through to the winter months. The projects are set within the different seasons, including fingerless gardening gloves to entice you outside in spring, the perfect beach bag to get you set for summer, a pair of cosy slippers to keep you warm as the weather turns to autumn and, finishing the year, is a wintry hot water bottle cover and festive holiday decorations. The projects are of varying complexity but each one is designed to be able to be completed within one week or even less. Similarly, the ideas range in scale from a winter-warmer scarf that takes seven balls of wool to cute Easter bunny egg cosies and a floral corsage that are both made from only oddments and so can help you to use up your yarn stash.

I hope you enjoy the designs in *The Knitter's Year*, both to make for yourself and to give as special handmade gifts. Why not makeover your home with the gingham cushion or decorative lace shelf edging? Or how about making the pumpkin pincushion or sewing needle case for a crafter friend? Or send your child back to school with their own unique pencil case to make the new autumn term a little brighter?

As with all my work, none of it would be possible without the huge support I get from great knitters, editors and pattern checkers, but I can honestly say that *The Knitter's Year* would not have come to fruition without the invaluable contribution of Rosy Tucker. Friend and colleague, she was there from the initial brainstorming and scribbling of lists in cafés, continuing with her design and practical input to the collection. I love the sheer joy of collaborating with other people and feel privileged to not only have had the opportunity to work once more with Rosy but also the fantastic team at Quadrille Publishing.

Debbie Bliss

Types of yarn

The yarns I have chosen for the designs in this book range from my organic cottons to cashmerinos and pure wools, each with their own contribution to make to the designs. It may be that they give crisp stitch detail in a simple pattern, such as the textured basket worked in aran-weight cotton, or provide softness and cosiness in a chunky scarf.

Unless you are using up your stash to make the smaller items in this book, make the effort to buy the yarn stated in the pattern. Each of these designs has been created with a specific yarn in mind.

A different yarn may not produce the same quality of fabric or have the same wash and wear properties. From an aesthetic point of view, the clarity of a subtle stitch pattern may be lost if a garment is knitted in an inferior yarn. However, there may be occasions when a knitter needs to substitute a yarn – if there is an allergy to wool, for example – and so the following is a guideline to making the most informed choices.

Always buy a yarn that is the same weight as that given in the pattern: replace a double knitting with a double knitting, for example, and check that the tension of both yarns is the same.

Where you are substituting a different fibre, be aware of the design. A cable pattern knitted in cotton when worked in wool will pull in because of the greater elasticity of the yarn and so the fabric will become narrower; this will alter the proportions of the garment.

Check the metreage of the yarn. Yarns that weigh the same may have different lengths in the ball or hank, so you may need to buy more or less yarn.

Here are descriptions of my yarns and a guide to their weights and types:

Debbie Bliss Baby Cashmerino:
- A lightweight yarn between a 4ply and a double knitting.
- 55% merino wool, 33% microfibre, 12% cashmere.
- Approximately 125m/50g ball.

Debbie Bliss Cashmerino Aran:
- An aran-weight yarn.
- 55% merino wool, 33% microfibre, 12% cashmere.
- Approximately 90m/50g ball.

Debbie Bliss Como:
- A super-chunky-weight yarn.
- 90% wool, 10% cashmere.
- Approximately 42m/50g ball.

Debbie Bliss Cotton DK:
- A double-knitting-weight yarn.
- 100% cotton.
- Approximately 84m/50g ball.

Debbie Bliss Eco Aran:
- An aran-weight yarn.
- 100% organic cotton.
- Approximately 90m/50g ball.

Debbie Bliss Eco Baby:
- A lightweight yarn between a 4ply and a double knitting.
- 100% organic cotton.
- Approximately 125m/50g ball.

Debbie Bliss Fez:
- An aran-weight yarn.
- 85% extra-fine merino wool, 15% camel.
- Approximately 100m/50g ball.

Debbie Bliss Rialto 4ply:
- A 4ply-weight yarn.
- 100% extra-fine merino wool.
- Approximately 100m/50g ball.

Debbie Bliss Rialto Aran:
- An aran-weight yarn.
- 100% extra fine merino wool.
- Approximately 80m/50g ball.

Debbie Bliss Rialto DK:
- A double-knitting-weight yarn.
- 100% extra fine merino wool.
- Approximately 105m/50g ball.

BUYING YARN

The ball band on the yarn will carry all the essential information you need as to tension, needle size, weight and yardage. Importantly it will also have the dye lot. Yarns are dyed in batches or lots, which can vary considerably. As your retailer may not have the same dye lot later on, buy all your yarn for a project at the same time. If you know that sometimes you use more yarn than that quoted in the pattern buy extra. If it is not possible to buy all the yarn you need with the same dye lot use the different ones where it will not show as much, on a neck or border, as a change of dye lot across a main piece will most likely show.

It is also a good idea at the time of buying the yarn that you check the pattern and make sure that you already have the needles you will require. If not buy them now, as it will save a lot of frustration when you get home.

ABBREVIATIONS

In a pattern book general abbreviations will usually be given at the front before the patterns begin, whilst those more specific to a particular design will be given at the start of the individual pattern. The following are the ones used throughout this book.

STANDARD ABBREVIATIONS

alt	alternate
beg	begin(ning)
cont	continue
dec	decrease(ing)
foll	following
garter st	garter stitch (k every row)
inc	increase(ing)
k	knit
kfb	knit into front and back of next stitch
m1	make one stitch by picking up the loop lying between the stitch just worked and the next stitch and working into the back of it
patt	pattern
p	purl
psso	pass slipped stitch over
rem	remain(ing)
rep	repeat(ing)
skpo	slip 1, knit 1, pass slipped stitch over
sl	slip
ssk	[slip 1 knitwise] twice, insert tip of left-hand needle from left to right through fronts of slipped stitches and k2tog
st(s)	stitch(es)
st st	stocking stitch
tbl	through back loop
tog	together
yf	yarn forward
yon	yarn over needle
yrn	yarn round needle

Spring

Basket

For those in need of extra storage space this charming knitted basket makes both a stylish and practical option. Worked in a textured knit and purl stitch pattern using a crisp cotton yarn, the knitted fabric is then lined and stiffened to achieve its rectangular shape. To complement the chocolate brown yarn, I have used a classic blue ticking as the lining fabric for the basket.

SIZE
18cm high x 27cm wide x 18cm deep

MATERIALS
Four 50g balls of Debbie Bliss eco aran in chocolate brown
Pair of 4.5mm knitting needles
100 x 30cm piece of buckram
67 x 58cm piece of cotton fabric for lining

TENSION
18 sts and 30 rows to 10cm square over patt using 4.5mm needles.

ABBREVIATIONS
See page 10.

NOTE
Basket is made in one piece.

TO MAKE
With 4.5mm needles, cast on 49 sts.
1st row (right side) K1, [p1, k1] to end.
2nd row P to end.
3rd row P1, [k1, p1] to end.
4th row P to end.
These 4 rows **form** the patt and are repeated.
Patt 2 rows.
** **Front handle**
Next row (right side) Patt 16, turn and cont on these sts only for first side of handle, p to end.
Patt 4 rows on these 16 sts, so ending with a p row, leave sts on a holder.
Next row With right side facing, rejoin yarn to rem 33 sts, cast off 17 sts, patt to end.
Patt 5 rows.
Next row (wrong side) P16, cast on 17 sts, p16 sts from holder. *49 sts.* **
Cont straight in patt until front measures 18cm from cast-on edge, ending with a right side row.
Foldline row (wrong side) K to end.
Shape for sides and base

Next row Cast on 34 sts, patt to end. *83 sts.*
Next row Cast on 34 sts, p to end. *117 sts.*
Cont in patt until work measures 36cm from original cast-on edge, ending with a p row.
Shape for back
Next row Cast off 34 sts, patt to end. *83 sts.*
Foldline row Cast off 34 sts, k to end. *49 sts.*
Cont in patt until work measures 50cm, ending with a wrong side row.
Back handle
Work as Front handle from ** to **.
Work a further 5 rows in patt, so ending with a right side row.
Cast off knitwise.

a smart, all-purpose
storage solution

TO MAKE UP

From buckram, cut two pieces 18 x 18cm
for ends and three pieces 18 x 27cm for sides
and base. Cut out the handle spaces in the two
side pieces. Attach the buckram pieces to the
knitted piece, if your buckram has an adhesive
side attach in this way or sew in place. Fold up
the knitted piece and join the edges.

LINING

From the fabric piece, cut out four 18.5 x
18.5cm squares, one from each corner, so leaving
a cross shape. Fold up the fabric (use the knitted
piece as a guide), then taking 1.5cm seam
allowances, join the sides of the cross. Make
a cut in the fabric sides for the centre of the
handles, snipping out from the ends of the cut
to the corners of the handle (see right), fold the
cut fabric onto the wrong side and press in place

to neaten the handle. Press 2cm around the
top edge onto the wrong side, place the lining
in the basket and slipstitch in place around the
handles and top edge.

HANDLE CUT OUT

KEY
---- cutting line

Lace cushion

As the days get warmer and longer, a crisp white cotton cushion provides perfect comfort when lounging outside in the spring sunshine. The cable and lace panel is knitted first and then sewn onto an existing cushion cover; I have contrasted the white lace panel against a charcoal grey cushion for maximum impact whilst the knitting is kept to a minimum. This project is a great way to practise your lacework skills as, unlike knitting a garment, you don't have to worry about shaping at the same time.

SIZE
Approximately 42cm square

MATERIALS
Two 50g balls of Debbie Bliss eco aran in white
Pair of 4.5mm knitting needles
Cable needle
46cm square fabric cushion cover and cushion pad

TENSION
19 sts and 25 rows to 10cm square over st st using 4.5mm needles.

ABBREVIATIONS
C3F slip next 2 sts onto cable needle and hold to front of work, k1, then k2 from cable needle.
C3B slip next st onto cable needle and hold at back of work, k2, then k1 from cable needle.
C3BP slip next st onto cable needle and hold at back of work, k2, then p1 from cable needle.
C3FP slip next 2 sts onto cable needle and hold to front of work, p1, then k2 from cable needle.
C4B slip next 2 sts onto cable needle and hold at back of work, k2, then k2 from cable needle.
C4F slip next 2 sts onto cable needle and hold to front of work, k2, then k2 from cable needle.
sk2togpo slip 1, k2tog, pass slipped st over.
Also see page 10.

PANEL PATTERN A
Worked over 19 sts.
1st row (right side) K1, [yf, ssk] 3 times, k5, [k2tog, yf] 3 times, k1.
2nd and every foll wrong side row Purl.
3rd row K2, [yf, ssk] 3 times, k3, [k2tog, yf] 3 times, k2.
5th row K3, [yf, ssk] 3 times, k1, [k2tog, yf] 3 times, k3.
7th row K4, [yf, ssk] twice, yf, sk2togpo, yf, [k2tog, yf] twice, k4.
9th row K5, [yf, ssk] twice, yf, sk2togpo, yf, k2tog, yf, k5.
11th row K6, [yf, ssk] twice, yf, sk2togpo, yf, k6.
13th row K7, [yf, ssk] 3 times, k6.

15th row K5, k2tog, yf, k1, [yf, ssk] 3 times, k5.
17th row K4, [k2tog, yf] twice, k1, [yf, ssk]
3 times, k4.
19th row K3, [k2tog, yf] 3 times, k1, [yf, ssk]
3 times, k3.
21st row K2, [k2tog, yf] 3 times, k3, [yf, ssk]
3 times, k2.
23rd row K1, [k2tog, yf] 3 times, k5, [yf, ssk]
3 times, k1.
24th row Purl.
These 24 rows **form** Patt Panel A and are
repeated.

PANEL PATTERN B
Worked over 17 sts.
1st row (right side) P1, C3FP, k2tog, yf, k3, yf,
ssk, k1, C3F, p2.
2nd row K2, p13, k2.
3rd row P2, C3FP, k2, k2tog, yf, k1, yf, ssk, k1,
C3F, p1.
4th row K1, p13, k3.
5th row P2, C3B, k1, k2tog, yf, k3, yf, ssk,
C3BP, p1.
6th row K2, p13, k2.
7th row P1, C3B, k1, k2tog, yf, k1, yf, ssk, k2,
C3BP, p2.
8th row K3, p13. k1.
These 8 rows **form** Patt Panel B and are
repeated.

CUSHION FRONT
With 4.5mm needles, cast on 77 sts.
Moss st row K1, [p1, k1] to end.

Rep this row 5 times more.
Foundation row (wrong side) Moss st 5, p19,
k1, p4, k4, p13, k2, p4, k1, p19, moss st 5.
Now work in patt as follows:
1st row (right side) Moss st 5, work across 19 sts
of 1st row of Patt A, p1, C4B, p1, work across
17 sts of 1st row of Patt B, p1, C4F, p1, work
across 19 sts of 1st row of Patt A, moss st 5.
2nd row Moss st 5, work across 19 sts of 2nd
row of Patt A, k1, p4, k1, work across 17 sts of
2nd row of Patt B, k1, p4, k1, work across 19 sts
of 2nd row of Patt A, moss st 5.
3rd row (right side) Moss st 5, work across 19 sts
of 3rd row of Patt A, p1, k4, p1, work across
17 sts of 3rd row of Patt B, p1, k4, p1, work
across 19 sts of 3rd row of Patt A, moss st 5.
4th row Moss st 5, work across 19 sts of 4th row
of Patt A, k1, p4, k1, work across 17 sts of 4th
row of Patt B, k1, p4, k1, work across 19 sts of
4th row of Patt A, moss st 5.
These 4 rows **form** the two 4-st cables and set
the position of the Patt Panels.
Working correct patt panel rows, cont in
patt until 3 repeats of the 24 rows of Patt
Panel A have been worked, so ending with a
wrong side row.
Work 5 rows in moss st.
Cast off in moss st.

TO FINISH
Position the knitted piece centrally on the
cushion cover front and slipstitch around
the edge. Insert cushion pad.

Flowerpot covers

Do your floral arrangements need smartening up for spring? Then why not knit some smart pot covers in delicate seasonal pastels? Moss stitch in leaf green, stocking stitch in pale pink and a fine cable rib in pale blue echo the shades of springtime blooms. All three covers are worked in simple stitches, which make them quick and easy to rustle up.

SIZE

Approximately 7cm high to fit 10–11cm diameter terracotta flowerpots

MATERIALS

One 50g ball of Debbie Bliss cotton dk in pale pink, apple green and duck egg
Pair of 4mm knitting needles
Cable needle (optional)

TENSION

20 sts and 28 rows over st st and 20 sts and 32 rows over moss st, both to 10cm square using 4mm needles.

ABBREVIATIONS

C2B slip next st onto cable needle and hold at back of work, k1, then k1 from cable needle or if working without the cable needle, k into front of 2nd st on left-hand needle, then k into front of 1st st and slip both sts off needle together.
Also see page 10.

RIB AND MOCK CABLE COVER

With 4mm needles and duck egg, cast on 46 sts.
1st row P2, [k2, p2] to end.
2nd row K2, [p2, k2] to end.
3rd row P2, [C2B, p2, k2, p2], to last 4 sts, C2B, p2.
4th row As 2nd row.
These 4 rows **form** the basic patt and are repeated.
Keeping patt correct and taking inc sts into k2, p2 rib, work a further 18 rows and inc 1 st at each end of 1st, 4th, 7th, 10th and 13th rows. *56 sts.*
Cast off in patt.

TO FINISH

Join seam and place around flowerpot.

STOCKING STITCH COVER

With 4mm needles and pale pink, cast on 39 sts. Beg with a k row, work 22 rows in st st and inc 1 st at each end of 3rd, 6th, 9th, 12th, 15th and 18th rows. *51 sts.*
Cast off.

TO FINISH

Join seam and place around flowerpot.

MOSS STITCH COVER

With 4mm needles and apple green, cast on 39 sts.
Moss st row K1, [p1, k1] to end.
Rep this row 23 times more and taking inc sts into moss st, inc 1 st at each end of 3rd, 6th, 9th, 12th, 15th and 18th rows. *51 sts.*
Cast off in moss st.

TO FINISH

Join seam and place around flowerpot.

pretty pastel
pot covers

Floral corsage

When I embarked on my career as a knitwear designer, I started out making hand-knitted plants so this floral corsage is a return to my design roots! If you are looking for a quick way to perk up an outfit, try this pretty rose in delicate shades of pink. For more of an impact, work the rose in vivid shades such as deep crimson with fuchsia or violet and mauve.

SIZE
Approximately 8 x 6cm
(including leaves)

MATERIALS
Small amounts of Debbie Bliss cotton dk in each of rose pink (A), pale pink (B) and apple green (C)
Pair each of 3.75mm and 4.5mm knitting needles
Brooch pin

ABBREVIATIONS
See page 10.

OUTER PETAL (MAKE 1)
With 4.5mm needles and A, cast on 81 sts.
K 1 row.
Next row P2, [k1, slip this st back on left-hand needle, lift next 10 sts one at a time over this st and off left-hand needle, slip st back onto right-hand needle] to last 2 sts, p2.
K 1 row.
Cut yarn and thread through rem 11 sts, pull up tightly and secure.

ROSE CENTRE (MAKE 1)
With 4.5mm needles and B, cast on 15 sts.
Beg with a k row, work 4 rows in st st.
Picot row (right side) With A, [k2tog, yf] to end.
Beg with a p row, work 4 rows in st st.
Cast off.
Fold in half along picot row and join cast-on to cast-off edge.

Join row ends.
Roll the strip around itself to form the rose centre and stitch to secure.

LEAVES (MAKE 2)
With 3.75mm needles and C, cast on 8 sts.
P 1 row.
Next row Skpo, k to last 2 sts, k2tog.
Rep the last 2 rows once more. *4 sts.*
P 1 row.
Next row Skpo, k2tog. *2 sts.*
P 1 row.
Next row K2tog and fasten off.

TO FINISH
Stitch rose centre in place to the centre of the outer petal. Arrange the leaves behind the flower and stitch in place. Attach a brooch pin.

a darling
rosebud brooch

Wash cloth

Knitted in my eco baby yarn – a Fairtrade organic cotton – this textured wash cloth takes less than an hour to make. Worked in reversible double moss stitch with a garter stitch edge, the finished cloth can be used as a wash cloth whilst bathing or as a dishcloth; either way, it couldn't be easier.

SIZE
Approximately 25cm square

MATERIALS
One 50g ball of Debbie Bliss eco baby in duck egg
Pair of 3.25mm knitting needles

TENSION
25 sts and 38 rows to 10cm square over double moss st using 3.25mm needles.

ABBREVIATIONS
See page 10.

TO MAKE
With 3.25mm needles, cast on 63 sts.
K 6 rows.
Next row (right side) K5, [p1, k1] to last 4 sts, k4.
Next row K4, [p1, k1] to last 5 sts, p1, k4.
Next row K4, [p1, k1] to last 5 sts, p1, k4.
Next row K5, [p1, k1] to last 4 sts, k4.
The last 4 rows **form** double moss st with garter st borders and are repeated.
Cont in patt until cloth measures 23cm from cast-on edge, ending with a wrong side row.
K 6 rows.
Cast off.

27

*cuddly and cosy
easter bunnies*

Bunny egg cosies

Keep your boiled eggs warm at Easter, and beyond. All three of the bunny egg cosies shown here are knitted from the same pattern, but with the simplest of embroidery their expressions range from puzzled to proud. In an assortment of colours, these small projects are a great way of using up oddments of yarn. Alternatively, you can make three the same from one single 50g ball.

SIZE
To cover a medium to large sized egg

MATERIALS
One 50g ball of Debbie Bliss rialto dk in main shade
Oddments of chocolate brown for embroidery
Pair of 3.25mm knitting needles

TENSION
24 sts and 40 rows to 10cm square over st st using 3.25mm needles.

ABBREVIATIONS
See page 10.

NOTES
Please note the egg cosy is worked with smaller than usually recommended needles for this yarn and the given tension reflects this.

TO MAKE
With 3.25mm needles, cast on 36 sts.
Beg with a k row, work 18 rows in st st.
Dec row [K2tog] to end. *18 sts.*
P 1 row.
Dec row [K2tog] to end. *9 sts.*
Cut yarn leaving a long length, thread through rem sts, pull up and fasten securely. Join seam, reversing at lower edge to allow for roll.

EARS (MAKE 2)
With 3.25mm needles, cast on 12 sts.
K 30 rows.
Dec row Skpo, k to last 2 sts, k2tog. *10 sts.*
K 1 row.
Rep the last 2 rows 4 times more. *2 sts.*
Next row K2tog and fasten off.
On cast-on edge, place a marker on 8th st for first ear and 4th st for second ear. Fold cast-on edge of each ear, matching edge of row to marked st, secure and then sew to head. With chocolate brown yarn, embroider eyes and nose as shown.

Bead necklace

This necklace is a pretty addition to any jewellery collection. In order to make it, all that is required is the ability to knit garter stitch – the simplest stitch of all – a few oddments of yarn, some wooden beads and a length of ribbon. I have used tonal pastel shades, but you could use stonger, more gem-like colours or alternate uncovered beads with those covered with knitting.

SIZE
Approximately 150cm long

MATERIALS
Oddments of Debbie Bliss eco baby in each of rose, pale pink, mauve and lilac
Pair of 3mm knitting needles
Approximately 150cm of 3mm wide satin ribbon
Nine 25mm beads
Darning needle

TENSION
25 sts and 34 rows to 10cm square over st st using 3.25mm needles.

ABBREVIATIONS
See page 10.

TIP
The covers fit snugly over the beads when worked on 3mm needles in garter stitch and stretched to its full extent. However, the stated tension is the recommended standard tension for this yarn, not the tension used.

TO MAKE
Make 3 in pale pink and 2 in each of rose, mauve, and lilac.
With 3mm needles, cast on 2 sts.
1st row [Kfb] into each st.
2nd row K to end.
Rep these 2 rows 3 times more. *32 sts.*
K 4 rows.
Next row [K2tog] to end.
Next row K to end.
Rep the last 2 rows 3 times more. *2 sts.*
Next row K2tog and fasten off.

TO FINISH
With a darning needle thread the ribbon through the beads. Place a knitted piece over each bead, in a repeating sequence of pale pink, mauve, lilac, rose, ending with pale pink, then join the side seam. Tie the ribbon to make the necklace, adjusting the length to suit.

a striking string of colourful beads

Bookmarks

An indispensible item for keen readers. It can be difficult to find something original to make to use up your leftover yarn, but these bookmarks fit the bill. You can work as many vertical lines as you like to create the woven effect so each one you make will look different. Use the delicate shades pictured here or brighter hues for a more vivid effect.

SIZE
Approximately 20cm long, excluding the tied yarn ends

MATERIALS
Oddments of Debbie Bliss baby cashmerino in silver (A), pale pink (B) and white (C)
Pair of 3.25mm knitting needles
Large-eyed blunt tipped sewing-up needle

TENSION
25 sts and 34 rows to 10cm square over st st using 3.25mm needles.

ABBREVIATIONS
See page 10.

TO MAKE
With 3.25mm needles and A, cast on 3 sts, leaving a long end.
K 1 row.
P 1 row.
Next row (wrong side) K1, m1, k1, m1, k1. *5 sts.*
P 1 row.
Next row K1, m1, k to last st, m1, k1. *7 sts.*
Rep the last 2 rows twice more. *11 sts.* **
Cont straight in st st until piece measures approximately 17cm from **, ending with a p row.
Next row K1, ssk, k to last 3 sts, k2tog, k1.
P 1 row.
Rep the last 2 rows until 5 sts rem, ending with a p row.
Next row K1, sl 2tog, k1, pass 2 slipped sts over, k1. *3 sts.*
P 1 row.
Next row K3tog and fasten off, leaving a long end.

TO FINISH
Working from the right (p) side, with lengths of B or C in the large-eyed needle, weave vertical lines into the stitches, leaving long ends at top and bottom. When all the lines have been woven in, tie the yarn ends into groups and trim. Press lightly.

Bow belt

The simplest garter stitch strip is embellished with spotty ribbon and a knitted bow to create this adorable belt. The ribbon ties at the back, making the belt fully adjustable, while contrast strips of garter stitch make a bow at the front. If you prefer a simpler look, leave off the knitted bow or tie the ribbon at the front.

SIZE
To tie around the waist

MATERIALS
One 50g ball of Debbie Bliss eco baby in silver grey (A) and small amount in white (B)
Pair of 3mm knitting needles
2m of 12mm wide petersham ribbon

TENSION
28 sts and 49 rows to 10cm square over garter st using 3mm needles.

ABBREVIATIONS
See page 10.

TIP
The length of the belt strip can be adjusted, if required, by knitting more or fewer rows, but as the ribbon extends beyond the length of the belt, this is not necessary.

BELT STRIP
With 3mm needles and A, cast on 10 sts and work in garter st (k every row) until strip measures 64cm.
Cast off.

BOW
With 3mm needles and B, cast on 14 sts and work in garter stitch for 20cm.
Cast off.

CENTRE STRIP
With 3mm needles and A, cast on 8 sts and work in garter stitch for 10cm.
Cast off.

TO MAKE UP
Place a marker in the centre of the belt strip. Fold the ribbon in half to find the centre, then matching the ribbon foldline to the marker, sew the ribbon along the length in the centre of the belt strip, leaving ribbon ends free. Join the cast-on and cast-off edges of the bow and with the seam at the centre back, sew in place to the centre of the belt strip. Join the cast-on and cast-off edges of the narrow centre strip, then slide this over the belt and the bow and sew in place to the back of the bow.

Sewing needle case

Knitted in duck egg blue cotton with chocolate brown and pale blue felt leaves, this sewing needle case is made using my all-time favourite colour combination. Lined with a smart striped cotton fabric, this case will keep your sewing needles safely tidied away.

SIZE
Approximately 11 x 9cm, when folded

MATERIALS
One 50g ball of Debbie Bliss eco baby in duck egg
Pair of 3mm knitting needles
18 x 12cm of fine cotton fabric for lining
Two pieces of 16 x 10cm felt

TENSION
26 sts and 40 rows to 10cm square over patt using 3mm needles.

ABBREVIATIONS
See page 10.

COVER
With 3mm needles, cast on 29 sts.
1st row (right side) K1, [p1, k1] to end.
2nd row P.
3rd row P1, [k1, p1] to end.
4th row P.
These 4 rows **form** the patt and are repeated.
Patt a further 32 rows, so ending with a 4th patt row.
Foldline row (right side) P.
Next row P.
Beg with a 3rd row, work 37 rows in patt, so ending with a 3rd patt row.
Cast off knitwise.

TO FINISH
Fold 1cm all around edge of lining fabric onto wrong side and press in place, folding in corners. Position lining centrally to wrong side of cover and slipstitch in place. Fold the two felt pieces in half and stitch together along the foldline, like pages in a book. Handstitch the felt 'pages' in place to the centre of the lined cover.

Baby cardigan
This pretty pastel top is knitted in single moss stitch, a reversible fabric that still looks great when the sleeve cuffs and collars are turned back. It is worked in my eco baby yarn, an organic cotton produced under the Fairtrade banner, that is kind to baby, the environment and the people who make it.

SIZES
To fit ages (in months)
3–6   6–9   9–12
Finished measurements
Chest
46   52   60cm
Length to shoulder
26   28   30cm
Sleeve length
12   14   16cm

MATERIALS
3 (4: 4) 50g balls of Debbie
Bliss eco baby in pale pink
Pair each of 3mm and 3.25mm
knitting needles
70cm of narrow ribbon

TENSION
25 sts and 42 rows to 10cm
square over moss st using
3.25mm needles.

ABBREVIATIONS
See page 10.

BACK
With 3.25mm needles, cast on
71 (81: 91) sts.
Moss st row K1, [p1, k1] to end.
This row **forms** moss st and is
repeated.
Cont in moss st until back
measures 14 (15: 16)cm from
cast-on edge, ending with a
wrong side row.

Dec row K1, [p3tog, yrn, k1, p1, sl 1, k2tog,
psso, yrn, p1, k1] to end. *57 (65: 73) sts.*
Cont in moss st until back measures 16 (17: 18)cm
from cast-on edge, ending with a wrong side row.
Shape sleeves
Cast on 38 (45: 52) sts at beg of next 2 rows.
133 (155: 177) sts.
Work straight until back measures 26 (28: 30)cm
from cast-on edge, ending with a wrong side row.
Next row Moss st 47 (57: 67), cast off next
39 (41: 43) sts for back neck, moss st to end.
Leave these 2 sets of 47 (57: 67) sts on holders.

LEFT FRONT
With 3.25mm needles, cast on 35 (41: 47) sts.
Work in moss st until front measures 14 (15: 16)cm
from cast-on edge, ending with a wrong side row.
1st size only
Dec row K1, p1, k1, [p3tog, yrn, k1, p1, sl 1,
k2tog, psso, yrn, p1, k1] to last 2 sts, p1, k1. *29 sts.*
2nd size only
Dec row K1, [p3tog, yrn, k1, p1, sl 1, k2tog,
psso, yrn, p1, k1] to end. *33 sts.*
3rd size only
Dec row K1, [p1, k1] twice, [p3tog, yrn, k1, p1, sl
1, k2tog, psso, yrn, p1, k1] to last 2 sts, p1, k1. *39 sts.*
All sizes
Cont in moss st until front measures 16 (17: 18)cm
from cast-on edge, ending with a wrong side row.
Shape sleeve
Cast on 38 (45: 52) sts at beg of next row.
67 (78: 91) sts.
Work straight until front measures 26 (28: 30)cm
from cast-on edge, ending with a wrong side row.
Next row Moss st 47 (57: 67), cast off next
20 (21: 24) sts. Leave sts on a holder.

RIGHT FRONT
With 3.25mm needles, cast on 35 (41: 47) sts.
Work in moss st until front measures 14 (15: 16)cm
from cast-on edge, ending with a wrong side row.
1st size only
Dec row K1, p1, k1, [p3tog, yrn, k1, p1, sl 1,
k2tog, psso, yrn, p1, k1] to last 2 sts, p1, k1. *29 sts.*
2nd size only
Dec row K1 [p3tog, yrn, k1, p1, sl 1, k2tog,
psso, yrn, p1, k1] to end. *33 sts.*
3rd size only
Dec row K1, [p1, k1] twice, [p3tog, yrn, k1, p1, sl
1, k2tog, psso, yrn, p1, k1] to last 2 sts, p1, k1. *39 sts.*
All sizes
Cont in moss st until front measures 16 (17: 18)cm
from cast-on edge, ending with a right side row.
Shape sleeve
Cast on 38 (45: 52) sts at beg of next row.
67 (78: 91) sts.
Work straight until front measures 26 (28: 30)cm
from cast-on edge, ending with a wrong side row.
Next row Cast off 20 (21: 24) sts, moss st to end.
Leave sts on a holder.

TO MAKE UP
Left shoulder Place sts on two needles with
points facing the cuff edge, then with right sides
together and wrong sides facing, knitting one
st from each needle together, cast off 14 (18:
22) sts, with one st on right-hand needle, turn
knitting so wrong sides are together and cast off
rem sts.
Right shoulder Work to match left shoulder.
Join side and underarm seams, reversing seam
on last 6 (7: 8)cm for cuff.
Thread ribbon through eyelets to tie at front.

freshen up shelves for springtime

Lace shelf edging

A pretty decorative edging adds some vintage style to an otherwise plain kitchen shelf. Knitted in a fine organic pure cotton, which gives great stitch detail, the lace pattern is worked over just 13 stitches and 12 rows so it and can be easily repeated until the edging is the length you require.

SIZE
Approximately 6.5cm at widest point

MATERIALS
One 50g ball of Debbie Bliss eco baby in white
Pair of 3.25mm knitting needles

TENSION
25 sts and 34 rows to 10cm square over st st using 3.25mm needles.

ABBREVIATIONS
y2rn yarn round needle twice.
Also see page 10.

NOTE
One 50g ball of eco baby will make a length of approximately 144cm.

TO MAKE
With 3.25mm needles, cast on 13 sts.
1st row (right side) K2, k2tog, y2rn, k2tog, k7.
2nd row K9, p1, k3.
3rd and 4th rows Knit.
5th row K2, k2tog, y2rn, k2tog, k2, [y2rn, k1] 3 times, y2rn, k2. *21 sts.*
6th row K3, [p1, k2] 3 times, p1, k4, p1, k3.
7th and 8th rows Knit.
9th row K2, k2tog, y2rn, k2tog, k15.
10th row K12 wrapping yarn twice round needle for each st, y2rn, k5, p1, k3.
11th row K10, [p1, k1] into next st, slip next 12 sts to right-hand needle, dropping extra loops, return sts to left-hand needle then k12tog. *13 sts.*
12th row Knit.
These 12 rows **form** the patt and are repeated until the edging is the length required, ending with an 11th patt row.
Cast off knitwise.

Gardener's gloves

Worked in fine cotton, with a contrast shade tipping the cuff and each finger and thumb end, these gloves are the perfect gift for any avid gardener. Because they are fingerless, they allow you to work on the more tricky tasks, such as pruning or tying up, but they are also pretty enough to wear outside of the garden too.

SIZES
To fit small/medium (medium/large) hands

MATERIALS
One 50g ball of Debbie Bliss eco baby in apple (M) and oddments of sage (C)
Pair each of 3mm and 3.25mm knitting needles

TENSION
25 sts and 30 rows to 10cm square over st st using 3.25mm needles.

ABBREVIATIONS
See page 10.

RIGHT GLOVE
** With 3mm needles and C, cast 42 (50) sts.
1st rib row (right side) K2, [p2, k2] to end.
Change to M.
2nd rib row P2, [k2, p2] to end.
These 2 rows form the rib and are repeated using M only.
Rib a further 17 rows.
Next row (wrong side) Rib to end and inc 8 sts evenly across row. *50 (58) sts.*
Change to 3.25mm needles.
Beg with a k row, work in st st throughout.
Work 8 rows **.
Shape thumb
Next row (right side) K25 (29), m1, k3, m1, k to end.
Work 3 rows.
Next row K25 (29), m1, k5, m1, k to end.

Work 1 row.
Next row K25 (29), m1, k7, m1, k to end.
Work 1 row.
Next row K25 (29), m1, k9, m1, k to end.
Work 1 row.
Cont to inc as set on 3 (4) foll right side rows, working 2 sts more between each inc, ending with a p row. *64 (74) sts.*
Divide for thumb
Next row (right side) K42 (48), turn.
Next row P17 (19), turn.
Work 6 rows in st st on these 17 (19) sts only.
Change to C.
Work 2 rows.
Cast off.
Join thumb seam.
With right side facing, join M to base of thumb, k to end. *47 (55) sts.*

Work 13 (15) rows in st st.

*** Divide for fingers

First (index) finger

Next row K30 (35), turn and cast on 2 sts.

Next row P15 (17), turn.

Work 6 rows in st st.

Change to C.

Work 2 rows.

Cast off.

Join seam.

Second (middle) finger

With right side facing, join M to base of first finger, pick up and k2 sts from cast-on sts at base of first finger, k6 (7), turn, cast on 2 sts.

Next row P16 (18), turn.

Work 8 rows in st st.

Change to C.

Work 2 rows.

Cast off.

Join seam.

Third (ring) finger

With right side facing, join M to base of second finger, pick up and k2 sts from cast-on sts at base of second finger, k6 (7), turn, cast on 2 sts.

Next row P16 (18), turn.

Work 6 rows in st st.

Change to C.

Work 2 rows.

Cast off.

Join seam.

Fourth (little) finger

With right side facing, join M to base of third finger, pick up and k2 sts from cast-on sts at base of third finger, k5 (6), turn.

Next row P12 (14).

Work 4 rows in st st.

Change to C.

Work 2 rows.

Cast off.

Join seam.

LEFT GLOVE

Work as given for Right Glove from ** to **.

Shape thumb

Next row K22 (26), m1, k3, m1, k to end.

Work 3 rows.

Next row K22 (26), m1, k5, m1, k to end.

Work 1 row.

Next row K22 (26), m1, k7, m1, k to end.

Work 1 row.

Next row K22 (26), m1, k9, m1, k to end.

Work 1 row.

Cont to inc as set on every alt row until there are 64 (74) sts on needle.

Work 1 row.

Divide for thumb

Next row K39 (45), turn.

Next row P17 (19).

Work 6 rows in st st.

Change to C.

Work 2 rows.

Cast off.

Join seam.

With right side facing, join M to base of thumb, k to end. *47 (55) sts.*

Work 13 (15) rows.

Complete as for Right Glove from *** to end.

Summer

Peg bag

To give your washing line a touch of style, knit this simple peg bag. It is worked in an aran-weight cotton, which knits up quickly and easily. The jaunty striped fabric lining adds a bright pop of colour.

SIZE
Approximately 31 x 25cm

MATERIALS
Three 50g balls of Debbie Bliss eco aran in duck egg
Pair of 4.5mm knitting needles
38 x 71cm piece of fabric for lining
30cm straight wooden clothes hanger

TENSION
20 sts and 30 rows to 10cm square over patt using 4.5mm needles.

ABBREVIATIONS
See page 10.

TIP
You may find it difficult to obtain 30cm coathangers, but you can cut a standard width hanger to size using a small hacksaw.

UPPER FRONT AND BACK
With 4.5mm needles, cast on 63 sts.
Next 2 rows K1, p1, turn, sl 1, p1.
Next 2 rows [K1, p1] twice, turn, sl 1, p3.
Next 2 rows [K1, p1] 3 times, turn, sl 1, p5.
Next 2 rows [K1, p1] 5 times, turn, sl 1, p9.
Next 2 rows [K1, p1] 7 times, turn, sl 1, p13.
Next 2 rows [K1, p1] 10 times, turn, sl 1, p19.
Next 2 rows [K1, p1] 13 times, turn, sl 1, p25.
Next row (right side) K1, [p1, k1] 31 times.
Next 2 rows P2, turn, sl 1, k1.
Next 2 rows P4, turn, sl 1, k1, p1, k1.
Next 2 rows P6, turn, sl 1, k1, [p1, k1] twice.
Next 2 rows P10, turn, sl 1, k1, [p1, k1] 4 times.
Next 2 rows P14, turn, sl 1, k1, [p1, k1] 6 times.
Next 2 rows P20, turn, sl 1, k1, [p1, k1] 9 times.
Next 2 rows P26, turn, sl 1, k1, [p1, k1] 13 times.
Next row P63.
Next row K1, [p1, k1] 31 times.
The last 2 rows **form** the pattern and are repeated.
Work straight in patt until upper front measures 10cm from cast-on edge, measured along the side edge and place a marker at each end of last row for top fold and mark the centre st of this row.

Cont straight in patt for a further 25cm for bag back, ending with a right side row.
Cast off knitwise.

LOWER FRONT
With 4.5mm needles, cast on 63 sts.
Next 2 rows K1, p1, turn, sl 1, p1.
Next 2 rows [K1, p1] twice, turn, sl 1, p3.
Next 2 rows [K1, p1] 3 times, turn, sl 1, p5.
Next 2 rows [K1, p1] 4 times, turn, sl 1, p7.
Next 2 rows [K1, p1] 5 times, turn, sl 1, p9.
Next 2 rows [K1, p1] 6 times, turn, sl 1, p11.
Next 2 rows [K1, p1] 7 times, turn, sl 1, p13.
Next 2 rows [K1, p1] 8 times, turn, sl 1, p15.
Next 2 rows [K1, p1] 10 times, turn, sl 1, p19.
Next 2 rows [K1, p1] 12 times, turn, sl 1, p23.
Next 2 rows [K1, p1] 14 times, turn, sl 1, p27.
Next row (right side) K1, [p1, k1] 31 times.
Next 2 rows P2, turn, sl 1, k1.
Next 2 rows P4, turn, sl 1, k1, p1, k1.
Next 2 rows P6, turn, sl 1, k1, [p1, k1] twice.
Next 2 rows P8, turn, sl 1, k1, [p1, k1] 3 times.
Next 2 rows P10, turn, sl 1, k1, [p1, k1] 4 times.
Next 2 rows P12, turn, sl 1, k1, [p1, k1] 5 times.
Next 2 rows P14, turn, sl 1, k1, [p1, k1] 6 times.
Next 2 rows P16, turn, sl 1, k1, [p1, k1] 7 times.
Next 2 rows P20, turn, sl 1, k1, [p1, k1] 9 times.

keep your pegs in line

Next 2 rows P24, turn, sl 1, k1, [p1, k1] 11 times.
Next 2 rows P28, turn, sl 1, k1, [p1, k1] 13 times.
Next row P63.
Next row K1, [p1, k1] 31 times.
The last 2 rows **form** the pattern and are repeated.
Work straight in patt until lower front measures 25cm from cast-on edge, measured along the side edge, ending with a right side row.
Cast off knitwise.

LINING
Join the cast-off edges of the two pieces together. Lay the knitted piece onto the lining fabric and draw around the edge (for the stitching line) adding a 1.5cm seam allowance around all edges. On the fabric, mark the position of the three upper front yarn markers. Fold the fabric matching the side yarn markers of the upper front to the stitching line points at the top of the lower front and join the seams, from the markers to the fold. Make 1cm snips into the curved edges of the lining, fold and press the seam allowances onto the wrong side.

TO MAKE UP
Matching the edges of the cast-on row of the lower front to the side edge yarn markers of the upper front, join the side seams of the knitted bag. Insert the lining into the bag and slipstitch the lining in place around the top edges. Make a small hole in the lining to accommodate the hook of the hanger. Insert the hanger hook through the small hole and the centre marked st of the upper front, fold the upper front over onto the lower front and stitch the sides, so forming the 'envelope'.

Tie on cushion

Give your chair a 1950s-style 'Doris Day' makeover with a gingham cushion that is far easier to knit than it looks. The back is worked in plain stocking stitch while the check pattern uses the stranding technique. For a bolder alternative colourway, I would recommend using a hot pink.

SIZE
Approximately 33cm square

MATERIALS
Three 50g balls of Debbie Bliss rialto aran in teal (A) and one 50g ball in each of duck egg (B) and ecru (C)
Pair of 4.5mm knitting needles
1m of 15mm wide tape
33cm square of 2cm thick foam sheet

TENSION
20 sts and 28 rows to 10cm square over st st using 4.5mm needles.

ABBREVIATIONS
See page 10.

COVER
Back
With 4.5mm needles and A, cast on 67 sts.
Beg with a k row, work 97 rows in st st, so ending with a k row.
Foldline row (wrong side) K.
Front
Now work in st st in colour patt as follows:
1st, 3rd and 5th rows (right side) K6A, [k5B, k5A] to last st, k1A.
2nd, 4th and 6th rows P6A, [p5B, p5A] to last st, p1A.
7th, 9th and 11th rows K6B, [k5C, p5B] to last st, k1B.
8th, 10th and 12th rows P6B, [p5C, p5B] to last st, p1B.
These 12 rows **form** the st st colour patt and are repeated 6 times more, then the first 6 rows again, so ending with a wrong side row.
P 1 row in A.
Cast off knitwise in A.

TO MAKE UP
Fold in half along foldline row and join side seams. Cut the tape in two equal lengths and fold each length in half and sew the fold to the wrong side of the open edge of the cushion back. Insert the foam pad and join the open edges together.

53

String bag
The humble string bag has been transformed into this super stylish carrier. I have given the bag a 'seaside' feel by working it in a bright white cotton yarn and edging it with nautical navy fabric binding.

SIZE
Approximately 56cm from base to top of strap when empty

MATERIALS
Three 50g balls of Debbie Bliss cotton dk in white
Pair each of 4.5mm and 9mm knitting needles
2m of 2.5cm wide bias binding

TENSION
There is no need to measure the tension as it is not important.

ABBREVIATIONS
See page 10.

TO MAKE
With 4.5mm needles, cast on 7 sts.
K 1 row.
Next row [Kfb] 6 times, k1. *13 sts.*
K 1 row.
Next row K1, [kfb, k1] to end. *19 sts.*
K 1 row.
Next row [Kfb] to last st, k1. *37 sts.*
K 1 row.
Next row K1, [kfb] to last st, k1. *55 sts.*
K 1 row.
Next row K1, [kfb, k2] to end. *73 sts.*
K 1 row.
Change to 9mm needles.
K 47 rows.
Next row K36, k2tog, k to end.
Divide for strap
Change to 4.5mm needles.
Next row K2tog, k32, k2tog, turn and cont on these 34 sts, leave rem 36 sts on a holder.
** K 1 row.
Next row K2tog, k to last 2 sts, k2tog.
Rep the last 2 rows until 10 sts rem.
K 60 rows.
Cast off. **
With correct side facing, rejoin yarn to first st on holder, k2tog, k to last 2 sts, k2tog.
Rep as first side of strap from ** to **.

TO FINISH
Join cast-off edges of strap together.
Join row ends of bag from strap divide to cast-on edge, then thread the yarn along cast-on edge, pull up and secure.
Fold the binding over all the row-end edges and stitch in place, folding the binding end under to neaten.

Baby sandals
As a change from the traditional baby socks or bootees, why not try a summery version with this take on the classic sandal? Worked in garter stitch and stocking stitch to create a firm fabric, the ankle strap slots through a loop at the front and then fastens with a button at the side.

SIZE
To fit ages 3–12 months

MATERIALS
One 50g ball of Debbie Bliss eco baby in navy
Pair of 2.75mm knitting needles
2 buttons

TENSION
25 sts and 34 rows to 10cm square over st st on 3.25mm needles.

ABBREVIATIONS
See page 10.

NOTE
The sandals are worked in garter stitch on smaller than usually recommended needles. The tension given is the standard for this yarn in stocking stitch, check your tension in stocking stitch first.

RIGHT SANDAL
With 2.75mm needles, cast on 36 sts and k one row.
1st row (right side) K1, yf, k16, yf, [k1, yf] twice, k16, yf, k1.
2nd and all wrong side rows K to end, working tbl into each yf of previous row.
3rd row K2, yf, k16, yf, k2, yf, k3, yf, k16, yf, k2.
5th row K3, yf, k16, yf, [k4, yf] twice, k16, yf, k3.
7th row K4, yf, k16, yf, k5, yf, k6, yf, k16, yf, k4.
9th row K5, yf, k16, yf, [k7, yf] twice, k16, yf, k5.
11th row K22, yf, k8, yf, k9, yf, k22. *64 sts.*
Shape instep
Next row K36, skpo, turn.
Next row Sl 1, p8, p2tog, turn.
Next row Sl 1, k8, skpo, turn.
Rep the last 2 rows 7 times more, then work first of the 2 rows again.
Next row Sl 1, k to end.
Next row K17, k2tog, p8, skpo, k17. *44 sts.*
Next row K24, turn.
Next row P4, turn.
Next row K4, turn.
Work 6cm in st st on these 4 sts only for front strap.
Cast off.

With right side facing, rejoin yarn at base of strap, pick up and k12 sts along side edge of strap. Turn and cast off knitwise all sts at this side of strap.
With right side facing, rejoin yarn to top of other side of strap, pick up and k12 sts along side edge of strap, then k rem 20 sts.
Cast off knitwise.
Join sole and back heel seam.
Place markers on 9th st at each side of back seam.
With right side facing and 2.75mm needles, pick up and k18 sts between markers along heel edge for ankle strap. **
Next row Cast on 22, k to end, turn and cast on 4 sts. *44 sts.*
Buttonhole row K to last 3 sts, k2tog, yf, k1.
K 2 rows.
Cast off.
Fold front strap over ankle strap to wrong side and slipstitch cast-off edge in place. Sew on button.

LEFT SANDAL
Work as given for Right Sandal to **.
Next row Cast on 4 sts, k to end, turn and cast on 22 sts. *44 sts.*
Buttonhole row K1, yf, skpo, k to end.
Complete as Right Sandal.

precious yet practical baby sandals

Pencil case

One of the pleasures of going back to school – or perhaps the only one – is the prospect of brand new pens, pencils and other stationery for the new school year. Send them back to class with their pencils packed away in this smart tartan zip-up case with a contrast fabric lining. Knit this pencil case over the summer holidays ready for the Autumn term.

SIZE
Approximately 9 x 23cm

MATERIALS
One 50g ball of Debbie Bliss rialto dk in each of teal (A) and mint green (B)
Pair of 4mm knitting needles
21 x 26cm piece of lining fabric
20cm zip fastener
Sewing thread and needle

TENSION
22 sts and 30 rows to 10cm square over st st using 4mm needles.

ABBREVIATIONS
See page 10.

TO MAKE
With 4mm needles and A, cast on 61 sts.
K 1 row.
Beg with a k row, work 22 rows in st st from chart 1 (see page 61), so ending with a p row.
K 3 rows in A only.
Beg with a p row, work 22 rows in st st from chart 2, so ending with a k row.
P 2 rows in A.
Cast off knitwise in A on wrong side row.

head back to
school in style

CHART 1

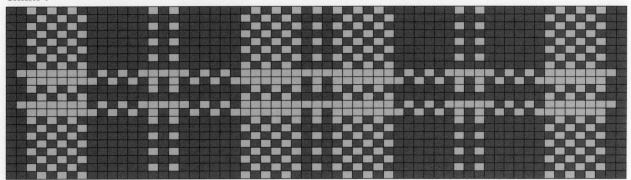

CHART 2

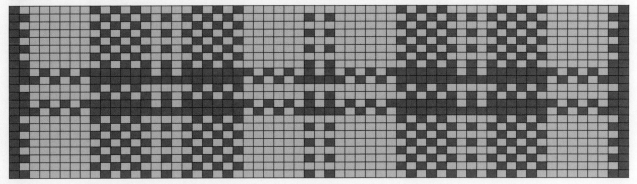

KEY
■ A teal
■ B mint green

TO MAKE UP
Fold knitting in half lengthways along central foldline and join side edges,
working mattress st through the centre of the edge st, leaving cast-on and cast-off
edges open. Join cast-on to cast-off edge, for approximately 1cm at each end. Pin,
tack and hand stitch zip in place.
Fold lining fabric in half lengthways and taking 1.5cm seams, join side seams,
from fold to raw edges, then continue to join top seam for approximately 1cm at
each end. Press 1cm around open edges onto wrong side. Insert lining into pencil
case and hand stitch lining to zip tape.
To assist opening and closing, cut a few lengths of yarn, thread through zip pull and
tie in a knot.

Lacy scarf

What could be simpler than this four-row lace pattern knitted in a crisp organic cotton to create the perfect summer scarf? The lovely openwork effect makes it light and delicate , while the two colour stripes of taupe and white add a touch of sophistication. The cast-on edge of the stitch pattern forms a decorative scalloped edge so the scarf is worked in two halves and joined in the middle to give this effect at both ends.

SIZE
Approximately 13 x 160cm (measured along side edge)

MATERIALS
Two 50g balls of Debbie Bliss eco baby in each of stone (A) and white (B)
Pair of 3.25mm knitting needles

TENSIONS
25 sts and 34 rows over st st and 29 sts and 32 rows over patt, both to 10cm square using 3.25mm needles.

ABBREVIATIONS
See page 10.

SCARF (MAKE 2)
With 3.25mm needles and A, cast on 38 sts.
Working in stripes of 4 rows A and 4 rows B, work in patt as follows:
1st row (right side) Knit.
2nd row Purl.
3rd row K1, * [k2tog] 3 times, [yf, k1] 6 times, [k2tog] 3 times; rep from * once more, k1.
4th row Knit.
Cont in 4 row stripes until scarf measures approximately 78cm from cast-on edge, ending with a 2nd row in A for one piece and 1st row in A for second piece.
Leave sts on a spare needle.

TO FINISH
With wrong sides together, hold the 2 needles side by side and with a 3rd needle work: k2tog (by taking one st from each needle and working them together each time), k2tog and pass first st over second st and off the needle, cast off all sts in this way, so joining the two pieces together.

Tealight covers
Pure white cotton covers slipped over translucent glass tumblers eminate the softest diffuse candlelight when filled with lit tealights. These knitted lacy bands are relatively straightforward to make, take just 7g of yarn each and really are a precious yet inexpensive gift.

SIZE
To fit a 7cm diameter straight sided glass tumbler

MATERIALS
One 50g ball of Debbie Bliss rialto 4ply in white (see NOTE)
Pair of 3.25mm knitting needles

TENSION
28 sts and 38 rows to 10cm square over st st using 3.25mm needles.

ABBREVIATIONS
See page 10.

NOTE
Oddments of yarn can be used as each cover weighs approximately 7g.

TO MAKE
With 3.25mm needles, cast on 19 sts.
1st row (right side) K18, yf, k1.
2nd row Cast off 1 st, k to end.
3rd row K8, [k2tog, yf] 4 times, k2, yf, k1.
4th row Cast off 1 st, k next 3 sts, [yrn, p2tog] 4 times, k7.
5th row K6, [k2tog, yf] 4 times, k4, yf, k1.
6th row Cast off 1 st, k next 5 sts, [yrn, p2tog] 4 times, k5.
7th row K4, [k2tog, yf] 4 times, k6, yf, k1.
8th row Cast off 1 st, k next 7 sts, [yrn, p2tog] 4 times, k3.
9th row K2, [k2tog, yf] 4 times, k8, yf, k1.
10th row Cast off 1 st, k next 9 sts, [yrn, p2tog] 4 times, k1.
These 10 rows **form** the patt and are repeated 7 times more.
Cast off.

TO FINISH
Join cast-on and cast-off edges.
Slip cover over glass tumbler making sure the top edge of the knitted piece sits well below top edge of the glass.

SAFTEY NOTE
Never leave lit candles unattended and keep away from children.

Lavender bags
Perfume your drawers or wardrobes with these sweet-smelling lavender-filled pyramids, knitted in moss stitch. Using summery pastel shades from my lightweight eco baby yarn, the unusual shape gives a contemporary twist to the traditional lavender sachet.

SIZE
Approximately 8cm high

MATERIALS
One 50g ball of Debbie Bliss eco baby in primrose, mauve or duck egg
Pair of 3mm knitting needles
Approximately 20g of dried lavender flowers for each bag
15cm of narrow ribbon (optional)

TENSION
26 sts and 45 rows to 10cm square over moss st using 3mm needles.

ABBREVIATIONS
See page 10.

TO MAKE
With 3mm needles, cast on 21 sts.
Moss st row K1, [p1, k1] to end.
Rep this row until piece measures 16cm.
Cast off.

TO MAKE UP
Join cast-on to cast-off edge to form a tube.
Flatten the tube at one end, with the seam centrally placed and join the row ends.
Flatten the open end of the tube and with the seam to one side, join the row ends, leaving approximately 4cm of the seam open.
Fill with dried lavender flowers and close the seam completely.
If you wish to hang the lavender bag, sew a loop of narrow ribbon to the top.

sweetly scented
lavender sachets

keep baby cool
in soft cotton

Striped baby hat
This simple beanie is my idea of a really relaxing knit as it can be whipped up in next to no time. But why stop at just one? Baby could have a different colour stripe combination for each day of the week. Made in cooling cotton, this hat takes little yarn and will protect baby's precious head from the sun's rays.

SIZE
To fit ages 6–12 months

MATERIALS
One 50g ball of Debbie Bliss
eco aran in each of teal (A) and
white (B)
Pair of 5mm knitting needles
Two 5mm double-pointed
knitting needles

TENSION
18 sts and 24 rows to 10cm
square over st st using 5mm
needles.

ABBREVIATIONS
See page 10.

TO MAKE
With 5mm needles and A, cast on 65 sts.
Beg with a k row, work 28 rows in st st (in
stripes of 4 rows A and 4 rows B alternately), so
ending with a p row.
Cont in st st and work 2 rows in B.
Shape top
Next row With B, k1, [k2tog, k6] 8 times. *57 sts.*
P 1 row in B.
Next row With A, k1, [k2tog, k5] 8 times. *49 sts.*
P 1 row in A.
Next row With A, k1, [k2tog, k4] 8 times. *41 sts.*
P 1 row in A.
Next row With B, k1, [k2tog, k3] 8 times. *33 sts.*
P 1 row in B.
Next row With B, k1, [k2tog, k2] 8 times. *25 sts.*
P 1 row in B.
Next row With A, k1, [k2tog] 12 times. *13 sts.*
P 1 row in A.

Next row With A, k1, [k2tog] 6 times. *7 sts.*
Do not cut yarn.

STALK
Slip rem 7 sts onto a 5mm double-pointed
needle.
Cont in A only and with right side facing, place
needle in left hand, pull yarn tightly from last st
to first st across wrong side and k7.
With right side still facing, slide these 7 sts
to the opposite end of the same needle, place
needle in left hand, pull yarn tightly from last st
to first st across wrong side and k7.
Rep the last row 4 times more.
Break yarn, leaving a long end, thread through
sts, pull up and secure.
Take yarn down through stalk and join seam in
hat, matching stripes.

Striped cushion

Stocking stitch stripes of taupe on a chalky white cushion cover will add a touch of elegance to a room. Work a single strip of knitting with simple buttonholes, sew up the side seams, add a few chunky buttons and… you're all done! As a variation on the theme, try white stripes on a taupe base.

SIZE
Approximately 35cm wide x
39cm high

MATERIALS
Three 50g balls of Debbie Bliss
cotton dk in white (A) and two
balls in stone (B)
Pair of 4mm knitting needles
35 x 35cm cushion pad
4 buttons

TENSION
20 sts and 28 rows to 10cm
square over st st using 4mm
needles.

ABBREVIATIONS
See page 10.

NOTE
The cushion cover is made in one piece, working
from the top edge of the Back, down to the
foldline, then up the Front to the top edge and
is fastened with 4 buttons.

TO MAKE
Cover back
With 4mm needles and A, cast on 70 sts.
Beg with a k row, work 9 rows in st st in A only,
so ending with a k row.
Beg with a p row, cont to work in st st in stripe
sequence as follows:
[2 rows in B, 2 rows in A] twice, 2 rows in B,
4 rows in A.
These 14 rows **form** the stripe patt and are
repeated 6 times more, so ending with a k row.
Cover front
Foldline row (wrong side) With A, k to end.
Beg with a k row, cont in st st, working in stripe
sequence as follows:

4 rows in A, [2 rows in B, 2 rows in A] twice,
2 rows in B.
These 14 rows **form** the stripe patt (a reverse of
the cover back) and are repeated 6 times more,
so ending with a p row.
Change to A and work 2 rows in st st.
Buttonhole row (right side) With A, k7, k2tog,
yf, k16, k2tog, yf, k16, yf, k2tog, k16, yf, k2tog,
k7.
Beg with a p row, work a further 6 rows in st st
in A only, so ending with a k row.
Cast off knitwise.

TO MAKE UP
Fold cover in half along the foldline row and
join the side seams, matching the stripes.
Sew buttons to the inside of the back to
correspond with the buttonholes.
Slip the cushion pad into the cover and fasten
the buttons.

Coat hanger

This simple covered coat hanger is the perfect starter project for a beginner knitter: work a straight strip of moss stitch in your chosen colour, stretch it over a padded hanger, sew in place and then finish it off with a decorative ribbon bow. Worked in an aran-weight cotton yarn, this really is a quick knit.

SIZE
To fit a 46cm plain wooden coat hanger

MATERIALS
One 50g ball of Debbie Bliss eco aran in white
Pair of 4.5mm knitting needles
Wadding
Plain wooden coat hanger
51cm of tape or ribbon (optional)

TENSION
19 sts and 30 rows to 10cm square over moss st
using 4.5mm needles.

ABBREVIATIONS
See page 10.

NOTE
Before beginning the cover, pad the hanger
with wadding and secure it in place with a
few stitches.

COVER
With 4.5mm needles, cast on 69 sts.
Moss st row (right side) K1, [p1, k1] to end.
This row **forms** moss st and is repeated throughout.
Cont in moss st until work measures approximately 12cm from cast-on edge.
Cast off in moss st.

TO MAKE UP
Fold the cover in half and join the row ends from fold to cast-on/cast-off edge.
Find the centre of the foldline and thread the hanger hook through the cover.
Stretch the cover over the padded hanger and join cast-on edge to cast-off edge.
Tie a length of tape or ribbon around the hook.

nautical but nice
summer holdall

Beach bag

The nautical look is always a favourite during the summer season. This rib and cable bag in knitted in the classic navy and white colourway, but its cheerful spot print lining gives it a modern edge. Whether you're on the deck of a cruise liner or heading to the beach, this bag is just right for carrying your holiday essentials.

SIZE
Approximately 40cm x 30cm x 9cm

MATERIALS
Six 50g balls of Debbie Bliss eco aran in navy (A) and one 50g ball in white (B)
Pair of 4.5mm knitting needles
Cable needle
2.5m of 4cm wide woven tape
140 x 30cm of buckram
60cm of 90cm wide non-stretch cotton lining fabric

TENSION
19 sts and 26 rows to 10cm square over st st using 4.5mm needles.

ABBREVIATIONS
C6F slip next 3 sts onto cable needle and hold to front of work, k3, then k3 from cable needle.
Also see page 10.

NOTE
The bag is worked in one piece.

TO MAKE
Front
With 4.5mm needles and A, cast on 110 sts.
1st row (right side) K2, [p2, k2] to end.
2nd row P2, [k2, p2] to end.
** Change to B and k one row.
4th row As 2nd row.
5th row As 1st row.
6th row As 2nd row.
Change to A and k one row **.
8th row As 2nd row.

Rep from ** to ** once more.
*** Cont in A only in patt as follows:
1st row (wrong side) [P2, k2] 4 times, [p6, k2, p2, k2] 7 times, [p2, k2] twice, p2.
2nd row [K2, p2] 4 times, [k6, p2, k2, p2] 7 times, [k2, p2] twice, k2.
3rd row As 1st row.
4th row [K2, p2] 4 times, [C6F, p2, k2, p2] 7 times, [k2, p2] twice, k2.
5th–8th rows Rep 1st and 2nd rows twice more.
These 8 rows **form** the rib and cable patt and are repeated.
Cont in patt until bag measures 25cm from ***, ending with a wrong side row.
Shape for base
Cast off 11 sts at beg of next 2 rows. *88 sts.*
Cont in patt as set until base measures 9cm, ending with a wrong side row.

Back

Next row Cast on 11 sts and work [k2, p2] twice, k2, p1 across these sts, patt to end.

Next row Cast on 11 sts and work [p2, k2] twice, p2, k1 across these sts, patt to end. ****

110 sts.

Cont in patt as set until bag back measures 25cm from ****, ending with a wrong side row.

Change to B and k 1 row.

Next row (wrong side) P2, [k2, p2] to end.

Next row K2, [p2, k2] to end.

Next row P2, [k2, p2] to end.

Change to A and k 1 row.

Next row P2, [k2, p2] to end.

Change to B and k 1 row.

Next row P2, [k2, p2] to end.

Next row K2, [p2, k2] to end.

Next row P2, [k2, p2] to end.

Change to A and k 1 row.

Next row P2, [k2, p2] to end.

Next row Cast off in A, working p2tog across each pair of purl sts.

TO MAKE UP

Lay the piece, right side down, on a flat surface and starting at the base, pin the tape in place, so that it runs behind the second cable from the right hand edge, up the bag back, then leave approximately 51cm free for back handle (this length is adjustable), continue to pin in place behind the second cable from the left-hand edge down the bag back, across the base and up the bag front following the same cable, then leave approximately 51cm free for front handle, making sure it is the same length as the first handle and continue to pin in place down to the base to meet up with the beginning of the tape. Stitch tape in place along both edges and across the tape at the top of the bag. Cut away any excess tape at the base, where it crosses.

Join side seams of bag from cast-on/cast-off edges down to base, then sew cast-on/cast-off edges of base shaping to row ends of base with side seam placed centrally.

From buckram, cut two pieces 40 x 28cm for sides, two pieces 9 x 28cm for ends and one piece 9 x 40cm for base. Turn bag inside out and hand sew buckram to wrong side of bag.

LINING

From fabric, cut a piece 52 x 73cm. With right sides together, fold fabric in half across the width and taking 1.5cm seam allowances, join the side seams from fold to cut edges, press seams open. Open out and refold the lining to form the bottom corners so that the side seams match the original fold, then stitch across the points so the seams are 9cm long to match the width of the bag base. Trim away the excess seam allowance at the corners. Press a 2cm hem around the top edge onto the wrong side. Insert lining into bag and slipstitch in place around the edge.

Flags

Create your very own 'united nations' with these fun flags. As I live in the UK but spend a lot of time in the US, I feel an affinity with both the Union Jack and the Stars and Stripes. However, I have included the Greek flag too as a reminder of a wonderful recent holiday to Corfu. Each flag uses only scraps of the different colour yarns, plus one bamboo knitting needle to make an ideal flag pole.

SIZE
Approximately 16 x 10cm

MATERIALS
One 50g ball of Debbie Bliss rialto 4ply in each colour (or oddments)
UK red (A), white (B) and blue (C)
US red (A), white (B) and blue (C)
Greece pale blue (A) and white (B)
Pair of 3.25mm knitting needles
Oddments of cotton fabric for backing
One 5mm bamboo knitting needle for each flag (for display)

TENSION
28 sts and 38 rows to 10cm square over st st using 3.25mm needles.

ABBREVIATIONS
See page 10.

NOTE
Each flag is worked from a chart using the relevant colours.

TO MAKE
With 3.25mm needles, cast on 47 sts for US and Greek flags and 46 sts for UK flag.
Beg with a k row, work in st st from the relevant chart (see pages 80 and 81) until all chart rows have been completed.
Cast off.

TO MAKE UP
US flag
Following chart 1, Swiss darn the stars on completion.
All flags
Press lightly on the wrong side. Cut a piece of backing fabric slightly larger than the flag. With right sides together, lay the flag onto the backing fabric and pin in place. Handstitch the backing to the flag around the two long sides and the short side without the selvedge sts. Trim away the excess fabric around the stitched edges. Turn through and press. Fold the backing fabric to the inside, along the open edge, leaving the selvedge sts free, then slipstitch the backing fabric in place along the fold. Fold the selvedge sts of the flag onto the back of the flag and slipstitch to the backing, leaving both ends open, so forming a channel for the 'flag pole'. Insert the bamboo needle into the channel.

CHART 1 (US)

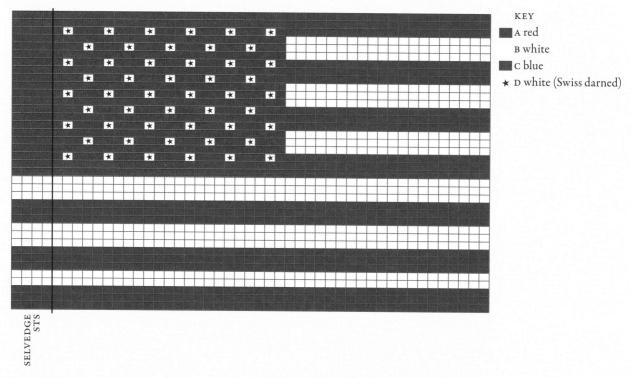

KEY
■ A red
  B white
■ C blue
★ D white (Swiss darned)

SELVEDGE
STS

CHART 2 (UK)

KEY
■ A red
  B white
■ C blue

SELVEDGE
STS

CHART 3 (GREECE)

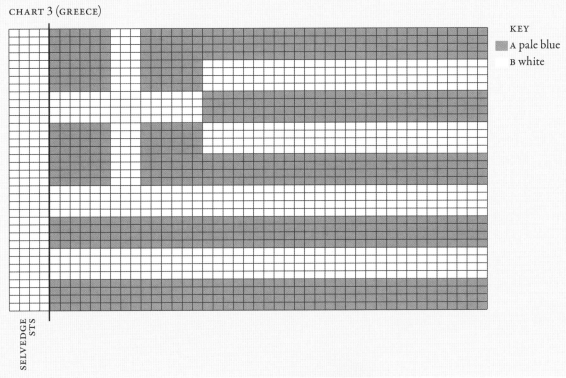

KEY
A pale blue
B white

SELVEDGE
STS

Autumn

Oddments knitting bag
Every knitter needs a holdall for their yarns, needles and work in progress. I can think of no better way of creating a knitting bag than to make it from your own stash. Working just two rows of garter stitch in each colour creates fine stripes. I used a combination of eight different colours, but you could use more or fewer shades depending on what leftover yarns you have to use up.

SIZE
Approximately 36cm wide at base and 30cm high

MATERIALS
Approximately 200g of Debbie Bliss rialto aran in assorted colours (see NOTES)
Pair of 4.5mm knitting needles
35cm of non-stretch cotton lining fabric
Sewing thread
Two 28cm lengths of bamboo cane (approximately 1cm diameter)

TENSION
20 sts and 44 rows to 10cm square over garter st using 4.5mm needles.

ABBREVIATIONS
See page 10.

NOTES
* I used one 50g ball of Debbie Bliss rialto aran in each of charcoal (A), cloud (B), toffee (C), gold (D), terracotta (E), light green (F), denim (G) and washed denim (H).
* If you use fewer colours or a single colour, you may use less yarn than the total stated.

FRONT AND BACK (BOTH ALIKE)
With 4.5mm needles and A, cast on 73 sts.
K 1 row.
Now work in 2-row repeating garter st stripes of B, C, D, E, F, G, H and A throughout, shaping as follows:
K 15 rows.
Dec row (wrong side) K14, k2tog tbl, k41, k2tog, k14. *71 sts.*
K 9 rows.
Dec row K14, k2tog tbl, k39, k2tog, k14. *69 sts.*
K 9 rows.
Dec row K14, k2tog tbl, k37, k2tog, k14. *67 sts.*
K 9 rows.
Cont in this way to dec 4 sts on every foll 10th row until 57 sts rem, ending with a dec row.
K 3 rows.
Shape for handles
Next row (wrong side) K20, cast off 17 sts, k to end and cont on this second set of 20 sts only, leave the first set of 20 sts on a holder.

K 1 row.
Next row (wrong side) K2, k2tog, k to end.
K 3 rows.
Rep the last 4 rows 5 times more, so ending with a right side row.
Cast off rem 14 sts knitwise.
With right side facing, rejoin yarn to 20 sts on holder, k to end.
Next row (wrong side) K to last 4 sts, k2tog tbl, k2.
K 3 rows.
Rep the last 4 rows 5 times more, so ending with a right side row.
Cast off rem 14 sts knitwise.

TO MAKE UP
Place markers on side edges, 21cm up from cast-on edge. Using one knitted piece as a template, cut two pieces of lining fabric, adding 1.5cm around all edges for seams and mark the position of the markers. Join the knitted pieces together along cast-on edges and side edges up to markers. Join fabric pieces together in the same way as the knitted pieces around the side and lower edges between the markers. Insert lining into bag and slipstitch around edges, leaving a gap at the top of the inner edge of the handle as shown. Insert bamboo canes for handles.

Cabled socks
Over-the-knee socks make a bold fashion statement, but they can also be worn rolled down – either way they keep toes cosy and are great for snuggling up in with a cup of hot chocolate and a favourite book. Knitted in my baby cashmerino yarn, the blend of merino wool, cashmere and microfibre makes them soft to the touch but hardwearing.

SIZE
To fit shoe size
UK 4–6/EUR 37–39

MATERIALS
Six 50g balls of Debbie Bliss baby cashmerino
in charcoal
Set of four 3.25mm double-pointed knitting
needles
Cable needle

TENSION
25 sts and 34 rows over st st and 32 sts and
34 rows over patt, both to 10cm square using
3.25mm needles.

ABBREVIATIONS
C2B slip next st onto cable needle and hold at
back of work, k1, then k1 from cable needle.
C2F slip next st onto cable needle and hold to
front of work, k1, then k1 from cable needle.
Also see page 10.

TO MAKE
With 3.25mm needles, cast on 88 sts.
Arrange sts onto 3 of the 4 needles.
Work in rounds of twisted rib as follows:
1st round [K1tbl, p1] to end.
Rep the last round for 8cm.
Inc row Rib 5, [m1, rib 8] to last 3 sts, m1, rib 3. *99 sts.*
Cont in patt as follows:
1st round [K1tbl, p2, k4, p2] to end.
2nd round As 1st round.
3rd round [K1tbl, p2, C2B, C2F, p2] to end.
4th round As 1st round.
These 4 rounds **form** the patt and are repeated.
Cont in patt until sock measures 34cm, ending with a 2nd round.
Dec round [K1tbl, p2tog, C2B, C2F, p2tog] to end. *77 sts.*
Cont in patt until sock measures 48cm, ending with a 3rd round.
Dec round [K1tbl, p1, k2, skpo, p1] to end. *66 sts.*
Cut yarn.
Shape heel
Re-arrange sts as follows: slip next 13 sts onto first needle, next 20 sts onto second needle, next 21 sts onto third needle and last 12 sts onto end of first needle.
Rejoin yarn to beg of first needle and work in rows as follows:
Next row (right side) K24, turn.

Next row Slip 1, p22, turn.
Next row Slip 1, k21, turn.
Next row Slip 1, p20, turn.
Cont in this way, working one less st on every row until the foll row has been worked:
Next row (wrong side) Slip 1, p10, turn.
Cont as follows:
Next row Slip 1, k11, turn.
Next row Slip 1, p12, turn.
Cont in this way, working one more st on every row until the foll row has been worked:
Next row Slip 1, p24, turn. **
With right side facing, slip next 25 sts onto first needle, next 20 sts onto second needle and next 21 sts onto third needle and work in rounds as follows:
Next round (right side) K25, p1, [k1 tbl, p1] to end of round.
Rep the last round until sock measures 16cm from **.
Next round K26, * [k2tog] twice, k1; rep from * to end. *50 sts.*

Shape toe
Next round [K1, skpo, k19, k2tog, k1] twice.
Next round K to end.
Next round [K1, skpo, k17, k2tog, k1] twice.
Next round K to end.
Next round [K1, skpo, k15, k2tog, k1] twice.
Next round K to end.
Cont in rounds decreasing on every alt round as set until the foll round has been worked:
Next round [K1, skpo, k7, k2tog, k1] twice. *22 sts.*
Slip first 11 sts onto one needle and rem 11 sts onto a second needle.
Fold sock inside out and cast off one st from each needle together.

89

Pan handler

If you are new to knitting and bored with endless practice samples, give yourself a sense of purpose by knitting up this practical saucepan or kettle handler. Bring a flash of colour into your kitchen by working it in a vivid shade such as the orange shown here. Whatever colour you choose, line the knitted piece with insulation and fabric and add a loop.

SIZE
Approximately 17 x 18cm

MATERIALS
One 50g ball of Debbie Bliss eco aran in orange
Pair of 4.5mm knitting needles
17 x 18cm piece of batting or felt (for added insulation)
19 x 20cm piece of cotton fabric (for backing)
13cm piece of ribbon

TENSION
19.5 sts and 26.5 rows to 10cm square over patt using 4.5mm needles.

ABBREVIATIONS
See page 10.

TO MAKE
With 4.5mm needles, cast on 33 sts.
1st and 10th rows K1, [p7, k1] to end.
2nd and 9th rows P1, [k7, p1] to end.
3rd and 12th rows K2, [p5, k3] to last 7 sts, p5, k2.
4th and 11th rows P2, [k5, p3] to last 7 sts, k5, p2.
5th and 14th rows K3, [p3, k5] to last 6 sts, p3, k3.
6th and 13th rows P3, [k3, p5] to last 6 sts, k3, p3.
7th and 16th rows K4, [p1, k7] to last 5 sts, p1, k4.
8th and 15th rows P4, [k1, p7] to last 5 sts, k1, p4.
These 16 rows **form** the pattern and are repeated twice more, casting off on the last 16th patt row.

TO FINISH
Catch stitch batting or felt piece in place to back of knitted piece. Press 1cm onto wrong side on all edges of fabric piece. Fold ribbon in half to form a loop, stitch ends together to hold in place and pin to one corner of fabric piece. Slipstitch fabric to backed knitted piece.

Pompon handwarmers
Keep your hands cosy but your fingers free with these cute handwarmers. Given in two sizes, to fit either an adult or a child, these fingerless mittens are worked in chunky rib in baby cashmerino and incorporate a contrast colour border. Perky pompons dangling from simple crochet cords, tied in a bow, finish them off.

SIZE
To fit 5–10 years (adult) hands

MATERIALS
One 50g ball of Debbie Bliss baby cashmerino in each of mid brown (A) and rose pink (B)
Pair of 3.25 knitting needles
3mm crochet hook
Large eyed, blunt-tipped sewing needle

TENSION
25 sts and 34 rows to 10cm square over st st using 3.25mm needles.

ABBREVIATIONS
See page 10.

TO MAKE (BOTH ALIKE)
With 3.25mm needles and A, cast on 42 (67) sts.
1st row (right side) P2, [k3, p2] to end.
2nd row K2 [p3, k2] to end.
These 2 rows **form** the rib pattern and are repeated throughout.
Work a further 38 (48) rows.
Shape thumb
Next row (right side) Rib 25 (38) sts, turn.
Next row Cast on 5 sts, rib 13 (14) sts, turn.
Cont on these 13 (14) sts only.
Rib 3 rows.
Change to B and rib a further 2 rows.
Cast off in rib.
Join thumb seam.
With right side facing, rejoin A at base of thumb and pick up and k3 (4) sts from 5 cast-on sts, then rib to end. *37 (62) sts.*
Rib 12 rows.
Change to B and rib a further 2 rows.
Cast off in rib.

TO FINISH
Join side seam.
With a crochet hook and B, make 2 chains approx 41cm long. Starting and finishing at the side seam, approx 4cm from cast-on edge, thread the chain through the ribs, with the large eyed needle.
With B, make 4 small pompons and attach one to each end of each chain.

Cabled moss stitch beret

I have knitted this beret in a classic shade of dark grey for a little continental chic. However, if grey feels like too much of a school uniform colour for your child, get them to choose an alternative hue. The cables are generously proportioned and provide textural contrast set against the moss stitch panels.

SIZE
To fit a 3–5 year old child

MATERIALS
Two 50g balls of Debbie Bliss rialto dk in charcoal
Pair of 4mm knitting needles
Two 3.25mm double-pointed knitting needles
Cable needle

TENSION
22 sts and 40 rows to 10cm square over moss st using 4mm needles.

ABBREVIATIONS
C4B slip next 2 sts onto cable needle and hold at back of work, k2, then k2 from cable needle.
pfb purl into front and back of next st.
pkp [p1, k1, p1] into next st.
Also see page 10.

TO MAKE
With 4mm needles, cast on 81 sts.
Moss st row K1, [p1, k1] to end.
Rep this row 4 times more.
Inc row K1, pkp, k1, [p2, pfb, p2, k1, pkp, k1, pkp, k1] to end. *121 sts.*
1st row (right side) [K1, p1] 3 times, k4, * p1, [k1, p1] 5 times, k4; rep from * to last 6 sts, [p1, k1] 3 times.
2nd row [K1, p1] 3 times, p4, * p1, [k1, p1] 5 times, p4; rep from * to last 6 sts, [p1, k1] 3 times.
3rd row [K1, p1] 3 times, C4B, * p1, [k1, p1] 5 times, C4B; rep from * to last 6 sts, [p1, k1] 3 times.
4th row As 2nd row.
Shape beret
Inc row Moss st 6, m1, k4, m1, * moss st 11, m1, k4, m1; rep from * to last 6 sts, moss st 6. *137 sts.*
Next row Moss st 7, p4, * moss st 13, p4; rep from * to last 7 sts, moss st 7.
Next row Moss st 7, C4B, * moss st 13, C4B; rep from * to last 7 sts, moss st 7.
Next row Moss st 7, p4, * moss st 13, p4; rep from * to last 7 sts, moss st 7.
The last 4 rows show the inc sts on one right side row and the cable crosses on the foll right side row, keeping the moss st and cable sts correct as set and taking inc sts into moss st, cont to inc 1 st at each side of every 4-st cable on 3 foll 4th rows until the foll row has been worked:
Inc row (right side) Moss st 9, m1, k4, m1, * moss st 17, m1, k4, m1; rep from * to last 9 sts, moss st 9. *185 sts.*

a cabled beret with continental chic

Keeping all sts correct, work 7 rows without further shaping.
Dec row (right side) Moss st 9, [k2tog, k2, ssk, moss st 17] 7 times, k2tog, k2, ssk, moss st 9. *169 sts.*
Next row Moss st 9, p4, [moss st 17, p4] 7 times, moss st 9.
Next row Moss st 9, C4B, [moss st 17, C4B] 7 times, moss st 9.
Next row Moss st 9, p4, [moss st 17, p4] 7 times, moss st 9.
Dec row (right side) Moss st 8, [k2tog, k2, ssk, moss st 15] 7 times, k2tog, k2, ssk, moss st 8. *153 sts.*
Cont in this way to dec 16 sts on every foll 4th row until 41 sts rem, ending with a dec row.
Next row K1, [p4, k1] 8 times.
Next row K1, [C4B, k1] 8 times.
Next row K1, [p4, k1] 8 times.
Dec row K2tog, [k2, k3tog] to last 4 sts, k2, k2tog. *25 sts.*
P 1 row.
Dec row K1, [k3tog] to end. *9 sts.*
P 1 row.
Dec row K1, [k2tog] 4 times. *5 sts.*
Do not cut yarn.

STALK
Slip rem 5 sts onto a 3.25mm double pointed needle and hold in left hand, then with right side facing, pull yarn firmly from last st to first st across wrong side and k5.
With right side still facing, slide these 5 sts to the opposite end of the same needle, place needle in left hand, pull yarn tightly from last st to first st across wrong side and k5.
Rep the last row 6 times more.
Leaving a 30cm yarn end, cut the yarn, thread through sts, pull up and secure. Using a blunt-tipped sewing-up needle, pass the yarn down through the centre of the stalk, then join the seam down to the cast-on edge.

Tea cosy

There was a period in my childhood when, at every teatime, no self-respecting teapot was without its pleated cosy. Usually these cosies were knitted in combinations of various sickly shades, so in homage to my favourite beverage here is my take on the retro tea cosy in a striking, clashing pairing of rust and pink.

SIZE
To fit a standard six-cup
'Brown Betty' teapot

MATERIALS
Two 50g balls of Debbie Bliss
rialto dk in each of fuchsia
(A) and rust (B)
Pair of 4mm knitting needles

TENSION
22 sts and 28 rows to 10cm
square over st st using 4mm
needles.

ABBREVIATIONS
See page 10.

PATTERN NOTE
When working the patt, the
'puckers' are formed by pulling
the yarn not in use across the
wrong side of the work and
twisting the two yarns together
at the colour change between
the 2nd and 3rd stitch of
every row.

SIDES (MAKE 2)
With 4mm needles and A, cast on 112 sts.
K 1 row.
Change to B and k 2 rows.
Now work in patt as follows:
1st row (right side) K2A, twist yarns together,
[k9B, pull yarn A across back of work and k9A,
pull yarn B across back of work] 6 times, k2B.
2nd row K2B, twist yarns together, [bring yarn
B to front (wrong side) of work, take yarn A
to back (right side) of work, k9A, pull yarn B
across wrong side of work, bring yarn A to front
(wrong side) of work, take yarn B to back (right
side) of work, k9B, pull yarn A across wrong side
of work] 6 times, k2A.
These 2 rows **form** the patt and are repeated.
Cont in patt until work measures 15cm from
cast-on edge, ending with a wrong side row.
Shape top
Cont to twist yarns between 2nd and 3rd sts of
every row and pull yarn not in use across wrong
side of work and shape as follows:
1st dec row (right side) K2A, [with B, skpo,
k5B, k2tog B, with A, skpo, k5A, k2tog A] 6
times, k2B.
Next row K2B, [k7A, k7B] 6 times, k2A.
2nd dec row K2A, [with B, skpo, k3B, k2tog B,
with A, skpo, k3A, k2tog A] 6 times, k2B.
Next row K2B, [k5A, k5B] 6 times, k2A.

3rd dec row K2A, [with B, skpo, k1B, k2tog B,
with A, skpo, k1A, k2tog A] 6 times, k2B.
Next row K2B, [k3A, k3B] 6 times, k2A.
4th dec row K2A, [with B, sl 1, k2tog, psso,
with A, sl 1, k2tog, psso] 6 times, k2B.
Next row K2B, [k1A, k1B] 6 times, k2A. *16 sts.*
Next row [K2tog A, k2tog B] to end. *8 sts.*
Cut yarns, thread both yarns through rem sts,
pull up and secure.

TO MAKE UP
Join the two pieces together along the row ends,
leaving gaps in the seams for the spout and the
handle. Make a 4cm pompon using both yarns
and sew to top of cosy.

keep your cuppa
steaming hot

Mug cosy
Whether I am sipping tea, coffee, chocolate or any other hot beverage, I like to make sure my drink doesn't cool off too quickly and so a mug cosy is a great help in keeping it warm. Worked in a two-colour slip stitch pattern in a dk weight yarn, you can either match the colours of your mug cosy to your tea cosy or go for a stand-alone colourway to create a one-off.

SIZE
To fit a straight sided 10cm high mug with an external diameter of 8cm.

MATERIALS
Oddments of Debbie Bliss rialto dk in each of fuchsia (A) and rust (B)
Pair of 4mm knitting needles

TENSION
25 sts and 52 rows to 10cm square over patt using 4mm needles.

ABBREVIATIONS
wytb with yarn to back of work.
wytf with yarn to front of work.
Also see page 10.

COSY
With 4mm needles and A, cast on 63 sts.
K 1 row.
1st and 3rd rows (right side) With B, k3, [sl 1 wytb, k3] to end.
2nd and 4th rows With B k3, [sl 1 wytf, k3] to end.
5th and 6th rows With A, k to end.
These 6 rows **form** the patt and are repeated.
Cont in patt until work measures 8cm from cast-on edge, ending with a 5th row.
Cast off knitwise in A.

TO FINISH
Join row ends at top and bottom, leaving a large gap in the seam for the handle.

Door draught excluder

Textured blackberry stitch, a plaited cable and rib are a great pattern combination for this draught preventer worked in a practical dark grey in rialto aran, my soft but hardwearing extra-fine merino wool. Laying across the bottom of the door to block any cold gusts of air, it is the stylish solution to keeping the shivers away.

SIZE

Approximately 86cm long

MATERIALS

Three 50g balls of Debbie Bliss rialto aran in charcoal

5mm circular knitting needle

Cable needle

13 x 89cm piece of cotton fabric

Polystyrene beads for filling

TENSION

25 sts and 24 rows to 10cm square over patt using 5mm needles.

ABBREVIATIONS

C4B slip next 2 sts onto cable needle and hold at back of work, k2, then k2 from cable needle.

C4F slip next 2 sts onto cable needle and hold to front of work, k2, then k2 from cable needle.

kpk [k1, p1, k1] all into next st.

Also see page 10.

TO MAKE

With 5mm circular needle, cast on 228 sts.

1st row (right side) [P1, k2] twice, [p1, C4B, k2, p1, k2, p14, k2] 8 times, p1, C4B, k2, p1, [k2, p1] twice.

2nd row [K1, p2] twice, * k1, p6, k1, p2, k1, [kpk, p3tog] 3 times, k1, p2; rep from * 7 times more, k1, p6, k1, [p2, k1] twice.

3rd row [P1, k2] twice, [p1, k2, C4F, p1, k2, p14, k2] 8 times, p1, k2, C4F, p1, [k2, p1] twice.

4th row [K1, p2] twice, * k1, p6, k1, p2, k1, [p3tog, kpk] 3 times, k1, p2; rep from * 7 times more, k1, p6, k1, [p2, k1] twice.

These 4 rows **form** the patt and are repeated throughout.

Cont in patt until work measures 20cm from cast-on edge, ending with a wrong side row.

Cast off in patt.

LINER

Fold the fabric piece in half lengthways, then taking a 1.5cm seam allowance, join the long edges to form a tube. Join across one short end. Fill the tube with polystyrene beads, then stitch across the open end of the tube.

TO MAKE UP

Join cast-on edge to cast-off edge. With seam lying centrally, join across one short end. Insert the filled liner and close the remaining short end.

block out chilly
autumn breezes

Striped gloves

Knitted in simple stocking stitch, I have kept the fingers of these gloves plain in order to make them easy to knit. So the stripes are worked on the main part of the hand and, for added interest, continue on the turned back cuff. I like the sophistication of the citrus brights against the dark grey base colour but there are plenty more three-colour combinations that would work well; try pastel shades for completely different look.

SIZE
To fit small/medium (medium/large) hands

MATERIALS
One 50g ball of Debbie Bliss rialto 4ply in each of grey (A), citrus (B) and orange (C)
Pair each of 3mm and 3.25mm knitting needles

TENSION
28 sts and 36 rows to 10cm square over st st using 3.25mm needles.

ABBREVIATIONS
See page 10.

RIGHT GLOVE
** With 3.25mm needles and A, cast 58 (66) sts.
Cont in stripes of 2 rows A, 2 rows B, 2 rows A, 2 rows C throughout.
Rib row [K1, p1] to end.
This row **forms** rib.
Rib a further 23 rows.
Change to 3mm needles.
Work a further 24 rows.
Change to 3.25mm needles.
Beg with a k row, work in st st.
Work 14 rows. **
Thumb shaping
Next row (right side) K29 (33), m1, k3, m1, k to end.
Work 3 rows.
Next row K29 (33), m1, k5, m1, k to end.
P 1 row.
Next row K29 (33), m1, k7, m1, k to end.
P 1 row.
Next row K29 (33), m1, k9, m1, k to end.
P 1 row.
Cont to inc 2 sts as set on every right side row until there are 74 (84) sts.
P 1 row.
Cont in A only.

Divide for thumb
Next row (right side) K48 (54), turn, cast on 2 sts.
Next row P21 (23) sts.
Work 18 rows in st st.
Next row K1, [k2tog] to end. *11 (12) sts.*
Next row P1, [p2tog] to last 0 (1) st, p0 (1).
Break yarn, thread through rem 6 (7) sts, draw up tightly and join seam.
With right side facing and continuing stripe sequence, join yarn to base of thumb, k to end. *55 (63) sts.*
Work 15 rows, so ending 2 rows C (A).
Cont in A only.
*** Divide for fingers
First finger
Next row K35 (41), turn and cast on 2 sts.
Next row P17 (19), turn.
Work 22 rows in st st.
Next row K1, [k2tog] to end.
Next row P1, [p2tog] to last 0 (1) st, p0 (1).
Break yarn, thread through rem 5 (6) sts, draw up tightly and join seam.
Second finger
With right side facing, join yarn to base of first finger, pick up and k2 sts from base of first finger, k7 (8), turn, cast on 2 sts.

Next row P18 (20), turn.

Work 26 rows in st st.

Next row [K2tog] to end.

Next row P1, [p2tog] to last 0 (1) st, p0 (1).

Break yarn, thread through rem 5 (6) sts, draw up tightly and join seam.

Third finger

With right side facing, join yarn to base of second finger, pick up and k2 sts from base of second finger, k7 (8), turn, cast on 2 sts.

Next row P18 (20), turn.

Work 22 rows in st st.

Next row [K2tog] to end.

Next row P1, [p2tog] to last 0 (1) st, p0 (1).

Break yarn, thread through rem 5 (6) sts, draw up tightly and join seam.

Fourth finger

With right side facing, join yarn to base of third finger, pick up and k2 sts from base of third finger, k6 (6), turn.

Next row P14 (14).

Work 16 rows in st st.

Next row [K2tog] to end.

Next row P1, [p2tog] to end.

Break yarn, thread through rem 4 sts, draw up tightly and join seam, reversing first 24 rows for cuff.

LEFT GLOVE

Work as given for Right Glove from ** to **.

Thumb shaping

Next row K25 (29), m1, k3, m1, k to end.

Work 3 rows.

Next row K25 (29), m1, k5, m1, k to end.

P 1 row.

Next row K25 (29), m1, k7, m1, k to end.

P 1 row.

Next row K25 (29), m1, k9, m1, k to end.

P 1 row.

Cont to inc 2 sts as set on every right side row until there are 74 (84) sts on needle.

P 1 row.

Divide for thumb

Next row K44 (50), turn, cast on 2 sts.

Next row P21 (23) sts.

Work 18 rows st st.

Next row K1, [k2tog] to end. *11 (12) sts.*

Next row P1, [p2tog] to last 0 (1) st, p0 (1).

Break yarn, thread through rem 6 (7) sts, draw up tightly and join seam.

With right side facing, join yarn to base of thumb, k to end. *55 (63) sts.*

Work 15 rows, ending 2 rows C (A).

Cont in A only.

Complete as for Right Glove from *** to end.

Pumpkin pincushion

As a reminder that knitting can be incredible fun, work this pumpkin pincushion as a Hallowe'en gift for a crafter friend. But if pumpkins aren't their thing, this same pattern could be knitted in shades of red to make either an apple or a tomato.

SIZE
Approximately 9cm diameter x 9cm high, including stalk

MATERIALS
One 50g ball of Debbie Bliss rialto dk in orange (A) and oddments in green (B)
Pair of 3.75mm knitting needles
Two 3.75mm double-pointed knitting needles
Washable toy stuffing

TENSION
25 sts and 32 rows to 10cm square over st st using 3.75mm needles.

ABBREVIATIONS
See page 10.

PUMPKIN
With 3.75mm needles and A, cast on 7 sts.
1st row [Kfb] 7 times. *14 sts.*
2nd row Purl.
3rd row [K1, m1, k1] 7 times. *21 sts.*
4th row [P1, k1, p1] 7 times.
5th row [K1, m1, p1, m1, k1] 7 times. *35 sts.*
6th row [P2, k1, p2] 7 times.
7th row [K1, m1, k1, p1, k1, m1, k1] 7 times. *49 sts.*
8th row [P3, k1, p3] 7 times.
9th row [K3, p1, k3] 7 times.
10th row As 8th row.
11th row [K1, m1, k2, p1, k2, m1, k1] 7 times. *63 sts.*
12th row [P4, k1, p4] 7 times.
13th row [K4, p1, k4] 7 times.
14th row As 12th row.
15th row [K1, m1, k3, p1, k3, m1, k1] 7 times. *77 sts.*
16th row [P5, k1, p5] 7 times.
17th row [K5, p1, k5] 7 times.
18th row As 16th row.
19th row As 17th row.
20th row As 16th row.
21st row [K2tog, k3, p1, k3, k2tog] 7 times. *63 sts.*
22nd to 24th rows As 12th to 14th rows.
25th row [K2tog, k2, p1, k2, k2tog] 7 times. *49 sts.*
26th to 28th rows As 8th to 10th rows.
29th row [K2tog, k1, p1, k1, k2tog] 7 times. *35 sts.*
30th row [P2, k1, p2] 7 times.
31st row [K2tog, p1, k2tog] 7 times. *21 sts.*

32nd row [P1, k1, p1] 7 times.
33rd row [Sl 1, k2tog, psso] 7 times. *7 sts.*
Break yarn, thread through sts, pull up and secure.

LEAVES AND STALK
With 3.75mm needles and B, cast on 54 sts.
1st row [K3, sl 1, k2tog, psso, k3] 6 times. *42 sts.*
2nd, 4th and 6th rows Purl.
3rd row [K2, sl 1, k2tog, psso, k2] 6 times. *30 sts.*
5th row [K1, sl 1, k2tog, psso, k1] 6 times. *18 sts.*
7th row [Sl 1, k2tog, psso] 6 times. *6 sts.*
8th row P1, p2tog, p2tog, p1. *4 sts.*
Change to 3.75mm double-pointed needles.
Next row K4.
Next row Keeping right side facing, transfer needle into left hand, push sts to opposite end of needle, pull yarn tightly across wrong side and k4.
Repeat the last row 6 times more.
Break yarn, thread through sts, pull up and secure. Thread yarn down through the stalk and join row ends.

TO MAKE UP
Join side seam in pumpkin, leaving a 4cm gap. Stuff firmly and close gap in seam. With a length of B in a large-eyed needle, wind yarn along the 7 purl st gulleys, securing yarn at top and bottom of pumpkin. Arrange leaves and stalk on the top of the pumpkin and stitch in place. Work a few sts in B at the base of the pumpkin.

Gadget covers
Knitted covers in bold stripes are a colourful way of making sure you can find your Blackberry or iPod in a cluttered bag. The ribbed stitch pattern expands so the cover will fit a variety of different sized gadgets. It is a brilliant way of using up your scraps of yarn as one cover takes only a very small amount of each colour. So try out lots of colourways to make each gadget cover completely unique.

SIZE
Approximately 5cm x 11cm

MATERIALS
Oddments of Debbie Bliss baby cashmerino in each of brown, peach, green, turquoise, grey, rust and gold
Pair of 3mm knitting needles

TENSION
32 sts and 36 rows to 10cm square over rib using 3mm needles.

ABBREVIATIONS
See page 10.

TIP
You can use these basic instructions to make a cover for any version of the iPod or Blackberry, just adjust the cast-on stitch count and number of rows.

IPOD COVER
With 3mm needles and brown, cast on 33 sts.
1st row (right side) K1, [p1, k1] to end.
2nd row P1, [k1, p1] to end.
These 2 rows **form** the rib and are repeated.
Work in rib in stripes as follows: 4 rows brown, 2 rows gold, 2 rows peach, 3 rows turquoise, 2 rows grey, 1 row rust, 3 rows green, 2 rows brown, 3 rows gold, 2 rows peach, 2 rows rust, 1 row grey, 2 rows brown, 4 rows turquoise, 1 row green, 3 rows peach, 3 rows brown.
Cast off in brown.

TO MAKE UP
Join row ends matching stripes. Sew in all yarn ends neatly.

SIZE
Approximately 12cm x 5cm

MATERIALS
Oddments of Debbie Bliss baby cashmerino in each of brown, pink, green, turquoise, grey, rust, red and gold
Pair of 3.25mm knitting needles

TENSION
30 sts and 35 rows to 10cm square over rib using 3.25mm needles.

BLACKBERRY COVER
With 3.25mm needles and brown, cast on 33 sts.
Work rib as given for iPod Cover, but working the stripe sequence as follows:
4 rows brown, 3 rows pink, 2 rows green, 4 rows turquoise, 1 row grey, 2 rows brown, 2 rows rust, 2 rows red, 1 row pink, 2 rows gold, 2 rows brown, 3 rows green, 1 row rust, 2 rows grey, 2 rows turquoise, 1 row red, 3 rows pink, 1 row gold, 4 rows brown.
Cast off in brown.

TO MAKE UP
As iPod Cover.

Slippers
Knitted all in one piece, these slippers are worked in a supersoft camel and extra-fine merino blend yarn called fez – a little bit of luxury for your feet. The duck egg blue edging contrasts the chocolate brown garter stitch and, like the pompons, adds a bit of decorative detail.

SIZES
To fit shoe sizes
UK 4–5 (5–6)
EUR 37–38 (38–39)

MATERIALS
Two 50g balls of Debbie Bliss fez in chocolate (A) and one ball in duck egg (B)
Pair of 4.5mm knitting needles
4.5mm circular knitting needle

TENSION
21 sts and 38 rows to 10cm square over garter st using 4.5mm needles.

ABBREVIATIONS
s2togkpo slip 2 sts tog, k1, then pass 2 slipped sts over.
Also see page 10.

SLIPPER (MAKE 2)
1st side With 4.5mm needles and A, cast on 6 sts.
K 1 row.
Next row Cast on 7 sts, k to end. *13 sts.*
K 2 rows. Leave sts on needle.
2nd side With 4.5mm needles and A, cast on 6 sts.
K 2 rows.
Next row Cast on 7 sts, k to end. *13 sts.*
K 1 row.
Joining row (right side) K across 13 sts of 2nd side, cast on 7 sts, then k across 13 sts of 1st side.
Shape heel of sole
Next row K13, p1, k5, p1, k13.
Next row K14, m1, k5, m1, k14. *35 sts.*
Next row K13, p1, k7, p1, k13.
Next row K14, m1, k7, m1, k14. *37 sts.*
Next row K13, p1, k9, p1, k13.
Next row K14, m1, k9, m1, k14. *39 sts.*
Next row K13, p1, k11, p1, k13.
Next row K14, m1, k11, m1, k14. *41 sts.*
Place markers at each end of next row.
Next row K13, p1, k13, p1, k13.
Next row K41.
Rep the last 2 rows (from markers) 26 (30) times more, so ending with a wrong side row.
Shape toe
Next row K1, ssk, k to last 3 sts, k2tog, k1. *39 sts.*
Next row K12, p1, k13, p1, k12.
K 1 row.
Next row K12, p1, k13, p1, k12.
Next row K1, ssk, k to last 3 sts, k2tog, k1. *37 sts.*
Next row K11, p1, k13, p1, k11.
K 1 row.
Next row K11, p1, k13, p1, k11.
Next row K1, [ssk, k9] twice, k2tog, k9, k2tog, k1. *33 sts.*

Next row K10, p1, k11, p1, k10.
K 1 row.
Next row K10, p1, k11, p1, k10.
Next row K1, ssk, k to last 3 sts, k2tog, k1. *31 sts.*
Next row K9, p1, k11, p1, k9.
K 1 row.
Next row K9, p1, k11, p1, k9.
Next row K1, [ssk, k7] twice, k2tog, k7, k2tog, k1. *27 sts.*
Next row K8, p1, k9, p1, k8.
Next row K1, ssk, k6, ssk, k5, k2tog, k6, k2tog, k1. *23 sts.*
Next row K7, [p1, k7] twice.
Next row K1, ssk, k5, ssk, k3, k2tog, k5, k2tog, k1. *19 sts.*
Next row K6, p1, k5, p1, k6.
Next row K1, [ssk] twice, s2togkpo, k3, s2togkpo, [k2tog] twice, k1. *11 sts.*
Next row K3, [p1, k3] twice.
Next row K1, [ssk] twice, k1, [k2tog] twice, k1.
Cast off knitwise.

EDGING
To form top seam, join row ends from toe cast-off edge for approximately 11cm (or as required).
With right side facing, 4.5mm circular needle and B, pick up and k one st in every alternate row-end all around top edge of slipper.
Cast off knitwise.
Join cast-on edges of 1st and 2nd sides and edging to form back seam and sew row ends of sides to heel cast-on sts.

TO FINISH
With B, make 2 pompons and sew to top of slippers.

snuggly slippers for toasty toes

Cabled bag

A hot pink bag will add a splash of bright colour to your autumn season wardrobe. Knitted in my super-soft, super-chunky como yarn, the thickness of the wool makes the scale of the oversized cable and bobbles big and bold. Knitted from the base of the bag upwards, the cable runs up the side of the bag and then continues to forms the handles. To finish the bag, it is lined with a matching bright tartan fabric.

SIZE

Approximately 35cm x 24cm x 10cm (see NOTE)

MATERIALS

Seven 50g balls of Debbie Bliss como in fuchsia
Pair of 9mm knitting needles
Cable needle
1m of cotton fabric for lining
9 x 32cm piece of cardboard for base

TENSION

9 sts and 14 rows to 10cm square over st st using 9mm needles.

NOTE

The size given above is the approximate external size. As the yarn is bulky, the internal size will be smaller.

ABBREVIATIONS

MB (make bobble) [k1, p1] twice into next st, turn, k4, turn, p4, turn, k4, turn, sl 2, k2tog, pass 2 slipped sts over.
C3B slip next st onto cable needle and hold at back of work, k2, then k1 from cable needle.
C3F slip next 2 sts onto cable needle and hold to front of work, k1, then k2 from cable needle.
C3FP slip next 2 sts onto cable needle and hold to front of work, p1, then k2 from cable needle.
C3BP slip next st onto cable needle and hold at back of work, k2, then p1 from cable needle.
C4B slip next 2 sts onto cable needle and hold at back of work, k2, then k2 from cable needle.
C4F slip next 2 sts onto cable needle and hold to front of work, k2, then k2 from cable needle.
Also see page 10.

CENTRE PANEL (WORKED OVER 15 STS)

1st row P5, k2, MB, k2, p5.
2nd row K5, p5, k5.
3rd row P5, MB, k3, MB, p5.
4th row K5, p5, k5.
5th and 6th rows As 1st and 2nd rows.

7th row P4, C3B, p1, C3F, p4.
8th row K4, p3, k1, p3, k4.
9th row P3, C3B, p1, k1, p1, C3F, p3.
10th row K3, p3, k1, p1, k1, p3, k3.
11th row P2, C3B, [p1, k1] twice, p1, C3F, p2.
12th row K2, p3, [k1, p1] twice, k1, p3, k2.
13th row P1, C3B, [p1, k1] 3 times, p1, C3F, p1.
14th row K1, p3, [k1, p1] 3 times, k1, p3, k1.
15th row C3B, [p1, k1] 4 times, p1, C3F.
16th row P3, [k1, p1] 4 times, k1, p3.
17th row K2, [p1, k1] 5 times, p1, k2.
18th row P2, [k1, p1] 5 times, k1, p2.
19th row C3FP, [p1, k1] 4 times, p1, C3BP.
20th row K1, p2, [k1, p1] 4 times, k1, p2, k1.
21st row P1, C3FP, [p1, k1] 3 times, p1, C3BP, p1.
22nd row K2, p2, [k1, p1] 3 times, k1, p2, k2.
23rd row P2, C3FP, [p1, k1] twice, p1, C3BP, p2.
24th row K3, p2, [k1, p1] twice, k1, p2, k3.
25th row P3, C3FP, p1, k1, p1, C3BP, p3.
26th row K4, p2, k1, p1, k1, p2, k4.
27th row P4, C3FP, p1, C3BP, p4.
28th row K5, p5, k5.
29th to 34th rows As 1st to 6th rows.
These 34 rows **form** the centre panel.

BACK AND FRONT (BOTH ALIKE)

With 9mm needles, cast on 45 sts.

K 1 row.

Next row (wrong side) K9, p4, k19, p4, k9.

Work in patt as follows:

1st row (right side) [K1, p1] 3 times, k9, work across 15 sts of 1st row of centre panel, k9, [p1, k1] 3 times.

2nd row P1, [k1, p1] 3 times, k2, p4, k2, work across 2nd row of centre panel, k2, p4, k2, p1, [k1, p1] 3 times.

3rd row P1, [k1, p1] 3 times, k2, C4F, k2, work across 3rd row of centre panel, k2, C4B, k2, p1, [k1, p1] 3 times.

4th row K1, [p1, k1] 3 times, k2, p4, k2, work across 4th row of centre panel, k2, p4, k2, k1, [p1, k1] 3 times.

These 4 rows **form** the patt for the 4-st cable with double moss st at each side and set the position for the centre panel.

Cont in patt working correct panel rows until all 34 rows of centre panel have been worked.

Next row K9, C4F, k19, C4B, k9.

Next row K9, p4, k19, p4, k9.

Next row K to end.

Next row K9, p4, k19, p4, k9.

Next row Cast off 7 sts, with one st on needle after cast-off, k next st, C4F, k2, leave these 8 sts on a holder, cast off next 15 sts, with one st on needle after cast-off, k next st, C4B, k2, cast off rem 7 sts, leave second set of 8 sts on the needle.

Fasten off.

Handles

With wrong side facing, rejoin yarn to 8 sts on needle and work as follows:

** **1st row** (wrong side) K2, p4, k2.

2nd row K to end.

3rd row K2, p4, k2.

4th row K2, C4B, k2.

Rep the last 4 rows until strap measures 25cm, ending with a right side row.

Cast off **.

With wrong side facing and 9mm needles, rejoin yarn to 8 sts on holder and work from ** to **, working C4F instead of C4B.

GUSSET

With 9mm needles, cast on 13 sts.

K 4 rows.

1st row (right side) K1, [p1, k1] 6 times.

2nd row P1, [k1, p1] 6 times.

3rd row As 2nd row.

4th row As 1st row.

These 4 rows **form** the double moss st.

Cont in double moss st until gusset measures 85cm, ending with a wrong side row.

K 4 rows.

Cast off.

LINING

Using the knitted pieces as templates (excluding handles) and adding 1.5cm for seams all round, cut out lining fabric for back, front and gusset. Mark the handle positions on the back and front linings. Pin and tack the gusset to back and front around two short sides and one long edge, then stitch the seams, taking a 1.5cm seam allowance. Press 1.5cm onto wrong side around top edge. Cut out two pieces of lining fabric 54cm long by 7cm wide for handle linings. Cover the cardboard base in fabric.

TO MAKE UP

Stitch gusset in place to back and front, starting and finishing at top edge. Join cast-off edges of handles. For handle linings, press 1.5cm onto wrong side along both long edges, then place centrally to wrong side of knitted handles and slipstitch in place. Place lining inside bag and slipstitch top edge in place enclosing ends of handle lining. Slip covered cardboard base in place inside bag.

Winter

Chunky scarf
This scarf is generously long but knitted in como, a super chunky blend of merino wool and cashmere, and worked on large needles it really can be knitted up within one week. And because the weight of the como yarn means each stitch is well defined, the aran-style pattern of chevrons, moss stitch and bobbles really stands out.

SIZE
Approximately 22cm wide x 180cm long

MATERIALS
Seven 50g balls of Debbie Bliss como in grey
Pair of 6.5mm knitting needles
Cable needle

TENSION
10 sts and 15 rows to 10cm square over st st using 6.5mm needles.

ABBREVIATIONS
C3BP slip next st onto cable needle and hold at back of work, k2, then p1 from cable needle.
C3FP slip next 2 sts onto cable needle and hold to front of work, p1, then k2 from cable needle.
MB (make bobble) k into front, back and front of next st, turn and p3, turn and k3, turn and p1, p2tog, turn and k2tog.
T5BP slip next 3 sts onto cable needle and hold at back of work, k2, then p1, k2 from cable needle.
Also see page 10.

TO MAKE
With 6.5mm needles, cast on 27 sts.
1st row (right side) [K1, p1] twice, k3, p4, k2, p1, k2, p4, k3, [p1, k1] twice.
2nd row [P1, k1] twice, k7, p2, k1, p2, k7, [k1, p1] twice.
3rd row [P1, k1] twice, p7, T5BP, p7, [k1, p1] twice.
4th row [K1, p1] twice, k7, p2, k1, p2, k7, [p1, k1] twice.
5th row [K1, p1] twice, p6, C3BP, MB, C3FP, p6, [p1, k1] twice.
6th row [P1, k1] twice, k6, p2, k1, p1, k1, p2, k6, [k1, p1] twice.
7th row [P1, k1] twice, p5, C3BP, k1, p1, k1, C3FP, p5, [k1, p1] twice.
8th row [K1, p1] twice, k5, p2, k1, [p1, k1] twice, p2, k5, [p1, k1] twice.
9th row [K1, p1] twice, p4, C3BP, k1, [p1, k1] twice, C3FP, p4, [p1, k1] twice.
10th row [P1, k1] twice, k4, p2, k1, [p1, k1] 3 times, p2, k4, [k1, p1] twice.
11th row [P1, k1] twice, p3, C3BP, k1, [p1, k1] 3 times, C3FP, p3, [k1, p1] twice.
12th row [K1, p1] twice, k3, p2, k1, [p1, k1] 4 times, p2, k3, [p1, k1] twice.
13th row [K1, p1] twice, p2, C3BP, k1, [p1, k1] 4 times, C3FP, p2, [p1, k1] twice.
14th row [P1, k1] twice, k2, p2, k1, [p1, k1] 5 times, p2, k2, [k1, p1] twice.
15th row [P1, k1] twice, p1, C3BP, k1, [p1, k1] 5 times, C3FP, p1, [k1, p1] twice.
16th row [K1, p1] twice, k1, p2, k1, [p1, k1] 6 times, p2, k1, [p1, k1] twice.
These 16 rows **form** the cable and bobble patt with double moss stitch at each side and are repeated 15 times more.
Cast off.

*a plump pillow
in perfect plaid*

Tartan cushion

Guaranteed to brighten up any chair, this tartan cushion cover is worked in stocking stitch using the Fair Isle method of colourwork with the bright verticals embroidered on afterwards for ease. The back of the cushion cover is plain with a central button opening. The entire cover is knitted in rialto aran, my pure merino wool aran-weight yarn, so it knits up as quickly as possible.

SIZE
Approximately 35cm square

MATERIALS
Four 50g balls of Debbie Bliss rialto aran in navy (A), two 50g balls in red (B) and one 50g ball in gold (C)
Pair each of 4.5mm and 5mm knitting needles
3 buttons
35 x 35cm cushion pad

TENSION
21 sts and 28 rows to 10cm square over st st using 4.5mm needles.

ABBREVIATIONS
y2rn yarn round needle twice to make 2 sts.
Also see page 10.

CHART NOTES
When working from chart (see page 124), work right side rows from right to left as follows – k2 edge sts, [k across 20 sts of repeat] 3 times, then k15 edge sts; and work wrong side rows from left to right as follows – p15 edge sts, [p across 20 sts of repeat] 3 times, then p2 edge sts.
Work the first 2 rows, then work the 28-row repeat twice, then work the last 20 rows (78 rows worked in total).
Do not work the vertical stitches marked in C, as these will be Swiss darned on completion; when knitting from the chart, work these stitches in either A or B whichever is appropriate.

TO MAKE

With 4.5mm needles and A, cast on 77 sts.

K 6 rows.

P 1 row.

Buttonhole row (right side) K11, [k2tog, y2rn, ssk, k21] twice, k2tog, y2rn, ssk, k12.

Next row P, working [p1, p1 tbl] into each y2rn.

Beg with a k row, cont in st st until work measures 9cm, ending with a k row.

Change to 5mm needles.

Foldline row (wrong side) Knit.

Beg with k row, work 78 rows in st st from chart, see Chart Notes.

Change to 4.5mm needles and work in A only.

Foldline row (right side) Purl.

Beg with a p row, work in st st until cover measures 27cm from foldline row, ending with a k row.

K 4 rows.

Cast off knitwise on wrong side.

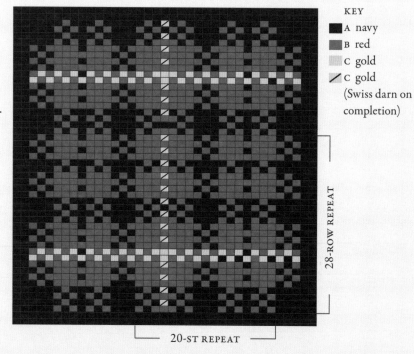

KEY

A navy
B red
C gold
C gold
(Swiss darn on completion)

28-ROW REPEAT

20-ST REPEAT

TO MAKE UP

Swiss darn the yarn C vertical lines following the chart.

Fold the larger part of the cover back onto the wrong side along the foldline row and join the side seams. Fold the remaining cover back along the foldline row and stitch the side seams.

Sew on the buttons to correspond with the buttonholes.

Slip the cushion pad into the cover and fasten the buttons.

Christmas napkin rings

Red napkin rings on crisp white linen – perfect! Simple knitted garter stitch strips are looped around each other, like a Russian wedding ring, to prove the maxim that less is more. These napkin rings bring an easy elegance to your Christmas table setting, and take only a few minutes to make.

SIZE
Each three-ring napkin ring will fit over a rolled standard napkin

MATERIALS
One 50g ball of Debbie Bliss rialto 4ply in red (see NOTES)
Pair of 3mm knitting needles

TENSION
32 sts to 10cm over garter st using 3mm needles.

ABBREVIATIONS
See page 10.

NOTES
* Oddments of yarn can be used as each ring weighs approximately 3g.
* Each napkin ring is made from three garter stitch strips.

TO MAKE (MAKE 3)
** With 3mm needles, cast on 45 sts.
K 4 rows, so ending with a right side row.
Cast off knitwise. **
Rep from ** to ** twice more.

TO MAKE UP
Join row ends of one strip to make a ring. Thread the second strip through the first ring and join the row ends in a ring. Thread the third strip through the other two strips and join the row ends in a ring.

KEY
■ 1ST RING
■ 2ND RING
■ 3RD RING

Bootee trio
These three pairs of bootees would make the most perfect gift set for any new baby. All three styles of bootee are worked from the same basic pattern: striped top with a roll-over cuff, striped sides with turned-up tops, or lace-edged with a bow. Smart or pretty, there is a pair for every occasion. Each design is knitted in baby cashmerino, my supersoft cashmere, merino and microfibre blend.

SIZE
To fit ages 3–6 months

MATERIALS
One 50g ball of Debbie Bliss baby cashmerino in each of red (A) and grey (B) (see NOTE)
Pair each of 2.75mm and 3.25mm knitting needles

TENSION
28 sts and 37 rows to 10cm square over st st using 2.75mm needles.

ABBREVIATIONS
See page 10.

NOTE
One 50g ball of each colour will make all three pairs of bootees.

BOOTEES WITH STRIPED INSTEP
** With 2.75mm needles and A, cast on 36 sts.
K 1 row.
1st row (right side) K1, yf, k16, yf, [k1, yf] twice, k16, yf, k1.
2nd and all wrong side rows K to end, working k1 tbl into each yf of previous row.
3rd row K2, yf, k16, yf, k2, yf, k3, yf, k16, yf, k2.
5th row K3, yf, k16, yf, [k4, yf] twice, k16, yf, k3.
7th row K4, yf, k16, yf, k5, yf, k6, yf, k16, yf, k4.
9th row K5, yf, k16, yf, [k7, yf] twice, k16, yf, k5.
11th row K22, yf, k8, yf, k9, yf, k22. *64 sts.*
12th row As 2nd row. **
Beg with a k row, work 10 rows in st st.
Shape instep
Next row With A, k36, skpo, turn.
Next row With A, sl 1, p8, p2tog, turn.
Cont in stripes of 2 rows B and 2 rows A and work as follows:

Next row Sl 1, k8, skpo, turn.
Next row Sl 1, p8, p2tog, turn.
Rep the last 2 rows 7 times more.
Cont in A only.
Next row Sl 1, k to end.
Next row P17, p2tog, p8, p2tog tbl, p17. *44 sts.*
Rib row [K1, p1] to end.
Rep the last row 9 times more.
Change to 3.25mm needles.
Work a further 12 rows in rib.
Cast off in rib.
Join back seam and sole seam.

BOOTEES WITH STRIPED FOOT

Work as given for Bootees with Striped Instep from ** to **.

Beg with a k row, work 5 rows in st st.

Next row (wrong side) [P next st tog with corresponding st 5 rows below] to end.

Beg with a k row, work 10 rows in st st, working in stripes of 2 rows B, 2 rows A.

Cont in A only.

Shape instep

Next row K36, skpo, turn.

Next row Sl 1, p8, p2tog, turn.

Next row Sl 1, k8, skpo, turn.

Rep the last 2 rows 7 times more, then work first of the 2 rows again.

Next row Sl 1, k to end.

Next row P17, p2tog, p8, p2tog tbl, p17. *44 sts.*

Rib row [K1, p1] to end.

Rep the last row 9 times more.

Rib 2 rows B, 2 rows A and 2 rows B.

With B, cast off in rib.

Join back seam and sole seam.

BOOTEES WITH LACY TOP

With B, work as given for Bootees with Striped Instep from ** to **.

With A, k 2 rows.

With B, beg with a k row, work 8 rows in st st.

With A, k 2 rows.

Cont in B only.

Shape instep

Next row K36, skpo, turn.

Next row Sl 1, p8, p2tog, turn.

Next row Sl 1, k8, skpo, turn.

Rep the last 2 rows 7 times more, then work first of the 2 rows again.

Next row Sl 1, k to end.

Next row P17, p2tog, p8, p2tog tbl, p17. *44 sts.*

Change to 3.25mm needles and cont in patt as follows:

1st row K2, [k2tog, yf, k1, yf, skpo, k2] to end.

2nd row P to end.

3rd row K1, [k2tog, yf, k3, yf, skpo] to to last st, k1.

4th row P to end.

These 4 rows **form** the patt.

Patt a further 12 rows.

With A, k 1 row.

With A, cast off knitwise.

Join back seam and sole seam.

Using 2 strands of B, make a twisted cord 46cm long for each bootee. Thread through first row of eyelet holes to tie at centre front.

Pompon garland

There really is nothing simpler – or more satifysing – than making pompons. In cool white, these giant pompons remind me of oversized snowballs; they make the simplest but most stylish seasonal decorations for winter time. Get the kids to help with winding the wool around the pompon maker then, once they are done, string each fluffy pompon onto a strand of yarn.

SIZE
Each pompon measures
9cm in diameter

MATERIALS
Five 50g balls of Debbie Bliss rialto dk in white
Pompon maker or cardboard for circles
Darning needle
Scissors

NOTE
Each pompon takes one 50g ball of yarn.

TO MAKE
If using cardboard, cut two identical 9cm diameter circles of cardboard.
Cut a 5cm diameter hole in the centre of each one and hold the circles together.
Thread a darning needle with yarn and wind it continually through the centre and outer edges until the hole has closed.
Insert the tips of the scissors between the two circles and cut the yarn around the circles. Tie a piece of yarn tightly between the two circles and remove the cardboard.

TO FINISH
With a darning needle, thread the pompons onto a length of yarn and make a loop at each end. Drape the line of pompons between two points.

Door stop

Keep the household traffic flowing with this great door stop. Knitted in tweed stitch – a sturdy variation of my favourite moss stitch – and made from a hardwearing, organic cotton in an aran weight, this robust fabric can put up with a lot of wear and tear.

SIZE

Approximately 16cm in each direction (this will change slightly when the door stop is filled)

MATERIALS

One 50g ball of Debbie Bliss eco aran in silver
Pair of 4.5mm knitting needles
Approximately 600g of small dried peas or beans

TENSION

24 sts and 36 rows to 10cm square over patt using 4.5mm needles.

ABBREVIATIONS

ytb yarn to back of work between two needles
ytf yarn to front of work between two needles.
pwise purlwise
Also see page 10.

DOOR STOP

With 4.5mm needles, cast on 39 sts.
1st row (right side) K1, [ytf, sl 1 pwise, ytb, k1] to end.
2nd row P2, [ytb, sl 1 pwise, ytf, p1] to last st, p1.
These 2 rows **form** the patt and are repeated throughout.
Cont in patt until work measures approximately 32cm from cast-on edge, ending with a right side row.
Cast off, work p2tog across the row, ending with p1.

LOOP

Cut three lengths of yarn 30cm long.
Fold each strand of yarn in half and plait the doubled yarn.
Fold the plait in half to form a loop and fasten off the ends.

TO MAKE UP

Join cast-on and cast-off edges together forming a tube (this seam will run along the centre of the base of the door stop).
Fold tube in half with the base seam lying centrally and join the seam from fold to fold (this seam will run across the front of the base of the door stop).
Refold the tube (forming a humbug shape) and with the plaited loop at the fold (top of door stop), join the seam from the fold towards the original base seam, leaving approximately 4cm of seam open.
Fill door stop with the dried peas or beans and close the seam.

*hold the door
with this
functional stopper*

*celebrate and spell out
the yuletide season*

Noel letters
This knitted 'noel' could take centre stage in your festive decorations year after year and become part of your family's Christmas customs. Backed by felt and stiffened with card, the letters are worked in a traditional Scandinavian style of Fair Isle in my 4ply rialto pure wool. You don't have to go for green; each of the letters could be knitted up in a different colour if you wanted to use up leftovers from your stash.

SIZE
The letters 'n', 'o' and 'e' are approximately 9.5cm high, while 'l' is 14.5cm high.

MATERIALS
One 50g ball of Debbie Bliss rialto 4ply in each of sage green (A) and ecru (B)
Pair of 3mm needles
30cm square of red felt
Cardboard
Double-sided tape

TENSION
32 sts and 36 rows to 10cm square over st st using 3mm needles.

ABBREVIATIONS
See page 11.

NOTES
All letters are made from straight strips using 3mm needles and are worked from charts. Read right side (k) rows from right to left and wrong side (p) rows from left to right.

N
With A, cast on 21 sts.
Beg with a k row, work 35 rows in st st from right-hand side of chart 1 (see page 138), so ending with a k row.
Leave sts on a holder.
With A, cast on 21 sts.
Beg with a k row, work 35 rows in st st from left-hand side of chart 1, so ending with a k row.
Joining row (wrong side) With A, p across 21 sts of second piece, then p across 21 sts on holder. *42 sts.*
Beg with a k row, work remaining 15 chart rows. Cast off all sts.

O
With A, cast on 42 sts.
Beg with a k row, work 10 rows in st st from chart 2 (see page 138).
Divide for centre hole
Next row (right side) K21 sts, turn and cont on these sts only, leave rem 21 sts on a spare needle.
Beg with a p row, work 24 rows from right-hand side of chart 2, so ending with a k row.
Leave sts on a holder.
Rejoin B yarn to sts on spare needle and k to end.
Beg with a p row, work 24 rows from right-hand side of chart 2, so ending with a k row.
Joining row (wrong side) With A, p across 21 sts of second piece, then p across 21 sts on holder. *42 sts.*
Beg with a k row, work remaining 15 chart rows. Cast off all sts.

E
With A, cast on 21 sts and work 94 rows in st st from main strip chart 4 (see page 140).
With A, cast on 14 sts and work 21 rows in st st from centre strip chart 5.

L
With A, cast on 21 sts and work 51 rows in st st from chart 3 (see page 138).
Cast off.

CHART 1 (N)

JOINING ROW

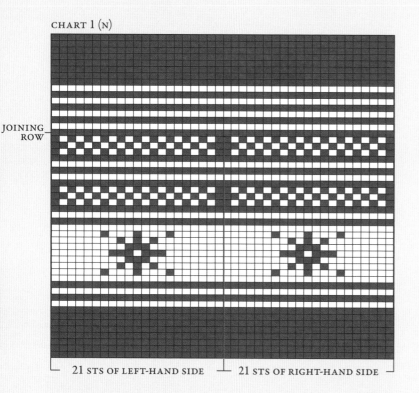

⌐ 21 STS OF LEFT-HAND SIDE ⌐ 21 STS OF RIGHT-HAND SIDE ⌐

TO MAKE UP

Cut out two pieces of card for each letter, using the templates on pages 140 and 141.

Cut out one piece of red felt for each letter, adding a 1.5cm allowance all around. Making sure you work with each letter in reverse, place the felt on one piece of card, fold the allowance over onto the back and attach it all around with double-sided tape. When working the upper part of the 'e', cut a small hole and clip around it so that the felt can be turned back over the card more easily.

Place the knitted pieces on the right side of the second card template for each letter, and with double-sided tape, attach the excess fabric to the back of the card, stretching and easing to fit where necessary. When working the 'e' first wrap the centre bar of card with the knitted centre strip, then wrap the remaining section of the card with the main strip and slipstitch where they join.

For each letter, place the wrong sides of the cards together and slipstitch around the edges.

CHART 2 (O)

CHART 3 (L)

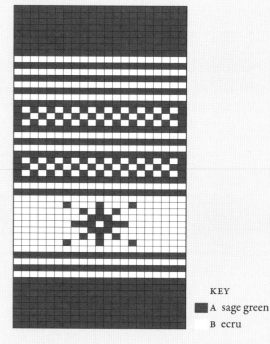

KEY

■ A sage green

□ B ecru

CHART 4 (E – MAIN STRIP)

CHART 5 (E – CENTRE STRIP)

KEY

A sage green

B ecru

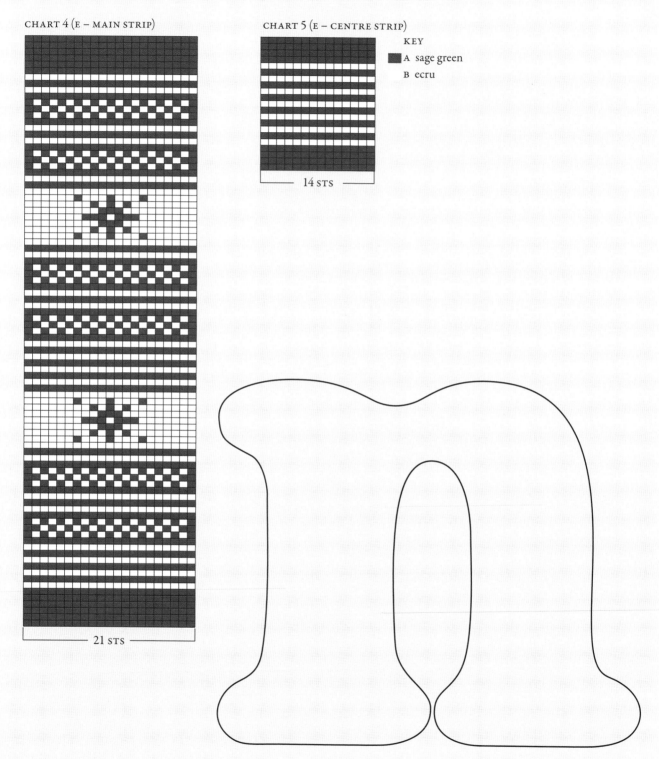

14 STS

21 STS

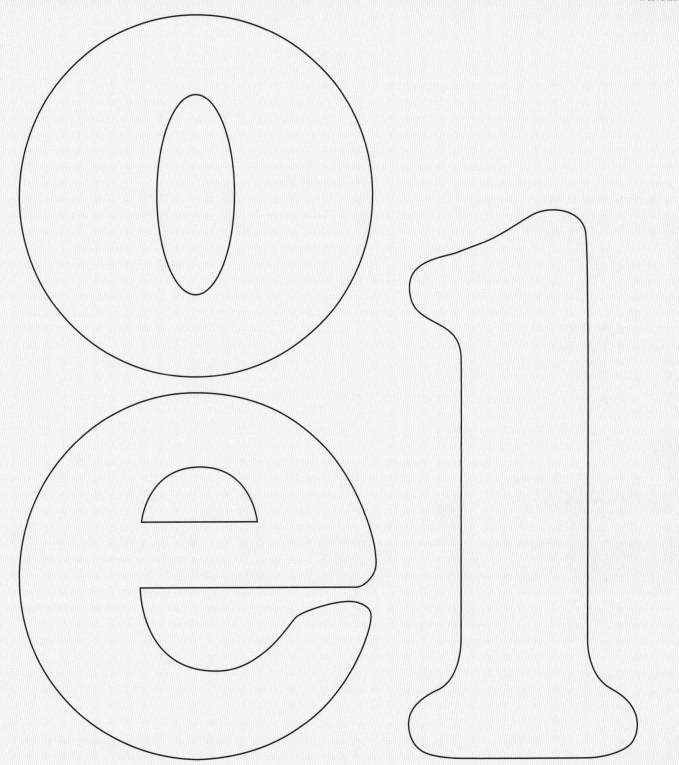

Hot water bottle cover

As winter draws in and the days become shorter, who doesn't love snuggling up of an evening under the eiderdown with a warming hot water bottle. This protective cover will stop you from getting scalded and help the hot water bottle retain its heat for longer. The simple drawstring shape of the cover means it is easy to knit as there is no need for any tricky shaping.

SIZE
To fit a standard sized hot water bottle

MATERIALS
Two 50g balls of Debbie Bliss cashmerino aran in stone
Pair each of 4mm and 5mm knitting needles
30cm of 12mm wide satin ribbon

TENSION
22 sts and 24 rows to 10cm square over patt (unstretched) using 5mm needles.

ABBREVIATIONS
See page 10.

TIP
You will need to insert the hot water bottle into the cover before filling.

FRONT
With 5mm needles, cast on 43 sts.
1st row (right side) [P1, k1] 3 times, * p2, k1, p1, k1, p2, [k1, p1] twice, k1; rep from * to last st, p1.
2nd and every foll wrong side row K all k sts and p all p sts as they appear.
3rd row P1, [k1, p1] to end.
5th row As 1st row.
7th row [K1, p1] twice, k1, * p2, [k1, p1] twice, k1, p2, k1, p1, k1; rep from * to last 2 sts, p1, k1.
9th row As 3rd row.
11th row As 7th row.
12th row As 2nd row.
These 12 rows **form** the front patt and are repeated 5 times more.
Change to 4mm needles.
Work 1st to 4th rows once.
Eyelet row (right side) P1, k1, yf, k2tog, p1, k1, p1, yon, skpo, p1, k1, p1, yon, k2tog, p1, k1, p1, yrn, p2tog, [p1, k1] twice, p1, p2tog, yrn, p1, k1, p1, skpo, yrn, p1, k1, p1, k2tog, yrn, p1, k1, p1, skpo, yf, k1, p1.
Next row [K1, p1] 3 times, * k2, p1, k1, p1, k2, [p1, k1] twice, p1; rep from * to last st, k1.
Change to 5mm needles.

Work 7th to 12th rows once.
Work 1st to 4th rows once more.
Cast off in patt.

BACK
With 5mm needles, cast on 43 sts.
[Work 7th to 12th rows as given for Front.
Work 1st to 12th rows as given for Front] 5 times, then work 1st to 6th rows once more.
Change to 4mm needles.
Work 7th to 10th rows once more.
Eyelet row K1, p1, k1, yf, skpo, p2, k1, yf, k2tog, p1, k1, p1, yon, skpo, p1, k1, p1, yon, k2tog, p1, k1, p1, skpo, yrn, p1, k1, p1, k2tog, yrn, p1, k1, p1, skpo, yf, k1, p2, k2tog, yf, k1, p1, k1.
Next row [P1, k1] twice, p1, * k2, [p1, k1] twice, p1, k2, k1, p1; rep from * to last 2 sts, k1, p1.
Work 1st to 10th row once more.
Cast off in patt.

TO MAKE UP
Join the two pieces around cast-on and side edges, leave top edge open. Thread ribbon through the eyelets and tie at centre front.

all good things
come in trees

Christmas tree decorations

Add some sparkle to the yuletide season with these beaded tree-shaped Christmas decorations; use them either as alternative ornaments for the tree or alongside the traditional baubles, tinsel and chocolate coins. Made in three separate sections and then threaded together to form the different branches of the fir tree, the beads are added on in the final stage to mimic festive baubles.

SIZE

Approximately 7 x 8cm, excluding ribbon loop

MATERIALS

Oddments of Debbie Bliss baby cashmerino in each of red, white and dark green
Pair of 3mm knitting needles
30cm of narrow ribbon for each tree
Assorted beads

TENSION

28 sts and 56 rows to 10cm square over garter st using 3mm needles.

ABBREVIATIONS

s2togkpo slip 2 sts together, k1, pass 2 slipped sts over.
Also see page 10.

LOWER SECTION

With 3mm needles, cast on 43 sts and k 2 rows.
Next row (right side) K9, [k2tog] twice, k17, [k2tog] twice, k9. *39 sts.*
K 1 row.
Next row K8, [k2tog] twice, k15, [k2tog] twice, k8. *35 sts.*
K 1 row.
** **Next row** K7, [k2tog] twice, k13, [k2tog] twice, k7. *31 sts.*
K 1 row.
Next row K6, [k2tog] twice, k11, [k2tog] twice, k6. *27 sts.*
K 1 row.
*** **Next row** K5, [k2tog] twice, k9, [k2tog] twice, k5. *23 sts.*
K 1 row.
Next row K4, [k2tog] twice, k7, [k2tog] twice, k4. *19 sts.*
K 1 row.
Next row K3, [k2tog] twice, k5, [k2tog] twice, k3. *15 sts.*
K 1 row.
Next row K2, [k2tog] twice, k3, [k2tog] twice, k2. *11 sts.*

K 1 row.
Next row K1, [k2tog] twice, k1, [k2tog] twice, k1. *7 sts.*
K 1 row.
Next row K2tog, s2togkpo, k2tog. *3 sts.*
K 1 row.
Next row S2togkpo.
Fasten off.

CENTRE SECTION

With 3mm needles, cast on 35 sts and k 2 rows.
Work as Lower Section from ** to end.

UPPER SECTION

With 3mm needles, cast on 27 sts and k 2 rows.
Work as Lower Section from *** to end.

TO MAKE UP

Join back seam in each section. Thread a length of ribbon up through the tip of each section, then leaving a loop of ribbon at the top of the upper section, thread the ribbon back through and tie the two ends together inside the lower section to secure. Sew beads to each section for tree baubles.

Christmas stocking

Worked in festive red and ecru, this Christmas stocking is knitted in, rather aptly, stocking stitch. The majority of the stocking has been kept plain, with the decorative colourwork stripes and snowflake motifs kept to a minimum. While it is small and simple enough to knit up in double-quick time, this stocking is big enough to hold all your surprise gifts and goodies.

SIZE
Approximately 46cm long

MATERIALS
Two 50g balls of Debbie Bliss rialto aran in red (A) and one 50g ball in ecru (B)
Pair each of 4.5mm and 5mm knitting needles
20cm of ribbon/tape for hanging loop

TENSION
18 sts and 24 rows to 10cm square over st st using 5mm needles.

ABBREVIATIONS
See page 10.

TO MAKE
With 4.5mm needles and A, cast on 65 sts.
K 1 row A, [k 2 rows B, k 2 rows A] twice, k 2 rows B.
Change to 5mm needles.
Beg with a k row, work 4 rows in st st in A.
Cont in st st and work 27 rows from chart 1 (see page 148).
Beg with a p row, work 30 rows in st st in A only.
Change to 4.5mm needles.
P 1 row.
Shape heel
First side
Next 2 rows K4, turn, sl 1, p3.
Next 2 rows K6, turn, sl 1, p5.
Next 2 rows K8, turn, sl 1, p7.
Cont to work shortened turning rows in this way until you have worked: K22, turn, sl 1, p21.
Next 2 rows K18, turn, sl 1, p17.

Next 2 rows K14, turn, sl 1, p13.
Next 2 rows K10, turn, sl 1, p9.
Next 2 rows K6, turn, sl 1, p5.
K 1 row across all sts.
Second side
Next 2 rows P4, turn, sl 1, k3.
Next 2 rows P6, turn, sl 1, k5.
Next 2 rows P8, turn, sl 1, k7.
Cont to work shortened turning rows in this way until you have worked: P22, turn, sl 1, k21.
Next 2 rows P18, turn, sl 1, k17.
Next 2 rows P14, turn, sl 1, k13.
Next 2 rows P10, turn, sl 1, k9.
Next 2 rows P6, turn, sl 1, k5.
Beg with a p row, work 5 rows in st st across all sts.
Change to 5mm needles.
Beg with a k row, work 9 rows in st st from chart 2 (see page 148).
Change to 4.5mm needles and work in A only.

147

CHART 1

CHART 2

KEY
■ A red
□ B ecru

Beg with a p row, work 7 rows in st st.
Shape toe
Next row (right side) K2, ssk, k25, k2tog, k3, ssk, k25, k2tog, k2.
Work 3 rows in st st.
Next row K2, ssk, k23, k2tog, k3, ssk, k23, k2tog, k2.
Work 3 rows in st st.
Cont in stripes of 2 rows B, 2 rows A alternately as follows:
Next row With B, k2, ssk, k21, k2tog, k3, ssk, k21, k2tog, k2.
P 1 row in B.
Work 2 rows in st st in A.
Next row With B, k2, ssk, k19, k2tog, k3, ssk, k19, k2tog, k2.
P 1 row in B.
Next row With A, k2, ssk, k17, k2tog, k3, ssk, k17, k2tog, k2.
P 1 row in A.

Next row With B, k2, ssk, k15, k2tog, k3, ssk, k15, k2tog, k2.
P 1 row in B.
Break B and cont in A only.
Next row K2, ssk, k13, k2tog, k3, ssk, k13, k2tog, k2.
Next row P2, p2tog, p11, p2tog tbl, p3, p2tog, k11, p2tog tbl, p2.
Next row K2, ssk, k9, k2tog, k3, ssk, k9, k2tog, k2.
Next row P2, p2tog, p7, p2tog tbl, p3, p2tog, k7, p2tog tbl, p2.
Next row K2, ssk, k5, k2tog, k3, ssk, k5, k2tog, k2.
Cast off.

TO FINISH
Join toe and back seam, matching patts and stripes. Fold ribbon/tape in half to form a loop and sew inside the top of the stocking.

Laced edged pillow

Perk up a plain pillowcase with a decorative lace edging. Some lace patterns can be challenging, but not this one as it is worked over just 6 stitches and a 4 row repeat. Knitted widthwise, the edging can be made as short or long as you like, so it can be used to trim any size of pillow or cushion. Worked in my eco baby, the organic cotton yarn gives the lace extra crispness and clarity of stitch.

SIZE
3cm wide at widest point

MATERIALS
One 50g ball of Debbie Bliss eco baby in white
Pair of 3.25mm knitting needles
One small pillowcase

TENSION
25 sts and 34 rows to 10cm square over st st using 3.25mm needles.

ABBREVIATIONS
y2rn yarn round needle twice to make 2 sts. Also see page 10.

TO MAKE
With 3.25mm needles, cast on 6 sts.
1st row (right side) K1, k2tog, yf, k2, y2rn, k1.
2nd row K2, k1 tbl, k2tog, yf, k3.
3rd row K1, k2tog, yf, k5.
4th row Cast off 2 sts, with 1 st on needle after cast-off, k2tog, yf, k3.
These 4 rows **form** the patt and are repeated.
Cont in patt until edging fits around the pillowcase approximately 2cm in from outer edge, allowing extra to ease at each corner, ending with a 3rd patt row. Cast off knitwise.

TO FINISH
Join cast-on and cast-off edges of edging, then beg at one corner, hand stitch the edging in place, easing in when turning the corners.

lovely lace pillows
for sweet dreams

Collared scarf

This combination of both a scarf and a collar rolled into one makes a witty fashion accessory. Worked in moss stitch – the perfect reversible fabric – it can be worn either as it is or tucked inside a neck opening for extra warmth. This scarf is knitted in cashmerino aran for absolute comfort and softness.

SIZE
Approximately 117 x 13.5cm

MATERIALS
Three 50g balls of Debbie Bliss cashmerino aran in stone
Pair of 5mm knitting needles
One button

TENSION
18 sts and 32 rows to 10cm square over moss st using 5mm needles.

ABBREVIATIONS
y2rn yarn round needle twice to make 2 sts.
Also see page 10.

TO MAKE
With 5mm needles, cast on 25 sts.
Moss st row K1, [p1, k1] to end.
Moss st a further 99 rows.
Next row Cast off 10 sts, moss st to end.
Moss st one row.
Next row Cast on 12 sts, moss st to end.
Moss st 170 rows.
Next row Cast off 12 sts, moss st to end.
Next row Moss st to end, turn.
Next row Cast on 10 sts, moss st to end.
Moss st 24 rows.
Buttonhole row Moss st 12, k2tog, y2rn, ssk, moss st to end.
Next row Moss st to end, working [k1, p1 tbl] into y2rn, moss st to end.
Moss st 74 rows.
Cast off.
Sew on button.

a perfect plum pudding beanie

Christmas pudding hat
Get in the festive mood by knitting up this cute baby's beanie with a rolled brim. Worked in an aran-weight yarn, there are only a few rows that involve a colour change so it is simpler to knit than it may appear. Picot edged leaves and bobble berries on the top complete the pudding.

SIZES
To fit ages 3–6 (6–12) months

MATERIALS
One 50g ball of Debbie Bliss rialto aran in each of chocolate (M) and ecru (C)
Small amounts of Debbie Bliss baby cashmerino in dark green for leaves and red for berries
Pair each of 3.25mm, 4mm and 5mm knitting needles   10   8

TENSION
18 sts and 24 rows to 10cm square over st st using 5mm needles.

ABBREVIATIONS
pwise purlwise
Also see page 10.

NOTE
When working with two colours, either use separate strands of yarn for each colour area, twisting yarns at colour change to avoid holes, or weave yarn not in use across wrong side where necessary in order to avoid long yarn floats.

TO MAKE
With 4mm needles and M, cast on 73 (81) sts.
Beg with a k row, work 12 rows in st st.
Change to 5mm needles.
Beg with a k row, work 22 (26) rows in st st.
Cont in st st and work in patt as follows (see NOTE):
1 **Next row** (right side) K 15 (17)M, 1C, 15 (17)M, 2C, 16 (18)M, 1C, 17 (19)M, 1C, 5M.
2 **Next row** P 4M, 3C, 4 (5)M, 1C, 11M, 1 (2)C, 6 (7)M, 1C, 8 (9)M, 3C, 8M, 1C, 6 (8)M, 2C, 3 (4)M, 1 (2)C, 10M.
3 **Next row** K 4M, 1C, 4 (5)M, 3C, 1 (2)M, 3C, 5 (7)M, 4C, 5M, 5C, 6M, 3 (4)C, 4 (5)M, 3 (4)C, 4 (3)M, 1C, 4 (5)M, 3C, 3 (4)M, 4C, 3M.
4 **Next row** P 2M, 6C, 1M, 5 (6)C, 2 (3)M, 3C, 2 (1)M, 5 (6)C, 2M, 5 (7)C, 3 (4)M, 8 (7)C, 3M, 6 (7)C, 3 (4)M, 8 (10)C, 3M, 3C, 3M.
5 **Next row** K2M, 5C, 1M, 10 (13)C, 1M, 19 (20)C, 1M, 34 (21)C, 0 (1)M, 0 (16)C.
Cont in C only.
P 1 row.
1 **Dec row** K1 (0), [k2tog, k7] 8 (9) times. *65 (72) sts.*
P 1 row.
3 **Dec row** K1 (0), [k2tog, k6] 8 (9) times. *57 (63) sts.*
P 1 row.
5 **Dec row** K1 (0), [k2tog, k5] 8 (9) times. *49 (54) sts.*
P 1 row.
7 **Dec row** K1 (0), [k2tog, k4] 8 (9) times. *41 (46) sts.*
P 1 row.

9 **Dec row** K1, [k2tog, k3] 8 (9) times. *33 (37) sts.*
10 **Dec row** [P2, p2tog] 8 (9) times, p1. *25 (28) sts.*
11 **Next row** K1 (0), [k2tog] to end. *13 (14) sts.*
12 **Next row** P1 (0), [p2tog] to end. *7 sts.*
Leaving approx 40cm, break off yarn, thread through rem sts, pull up and secure. Join seam, reversing seam at lower edge to allow the hem to roll.

LEAVES (MAKE 3)
With 3.25mm needles and dark green, cast on 21 sts.
Beg with a k row, work 4 rows in st st.
Picot row K1, [yf, k2tog] to end.
Beg with a p row, work 4 rows in st st.
Work cast-off as follows:
With right-hand needle, pick up the first st of the cast-on row, place it on left-hand needle and k tog with first st on left-hand needle, place next st from cast-on edge on left-hand needle and k tog with next st on needle, take first st on right-

hand needle over second to cast off; casting off sts in this way, cont to k each st tog with corresponding st of cast-on edge and cast off all sts. Fold in half and sew straight edges together.

BERRIES (MAKE 3)
With 3.25mm needles and red, cast on 1 st.
Next row [K1, p1, k1, p1, k1] all into st. *5 sts.*
K 1 row.
P 1 row.
Rep last 2 rows once more.
Next row K2tog, k1, k2tog. *3 sts.*
Next row Slip 1 pwise, p2tog, psso. *1 st.*
Fasten off, cut yarn and with a darning needle work a running stitch around edge of berry, draw up into a bobble and secure.

TO FINISH
Attach three leaves to the top of the hat and sew the berries in place to the centre.

Yarn Distributors

For stockists of Debbie Bliss yarns please contact:

UK & WORLDWIDE DISTRIBUTORS
Designer Yarns Ltd
Units 8–10
Newbridge Industrial Estate
Pitt Street, Keighley
W. Yorkshire BD21 4PQ, UK
t: +44 (0) 1535 664222
e: alex@designeryarns.uk.com
w: www.designeryarns.uk.com

USA
Knitting Fever Inc.
315 Bayview Avenue
Amityville
NY 11701, USA
t: +1 516 546 3600
w: www.knittingfever.com

CANADA
Diamond Yarns Ltd
155 Martin Ross Avenue
Unit 3
Toronto
Ontario M3J 2L9, Canada
t: +1 416 736 6111
w: www.diamondyarn.com

MEXICO
Estambres Crochet SA de CV
Aaron Saenz 1891–7
Col. Santa Maria, Monterrey
N.L. 64650, Mexico
t: +52 (81) 8335 3870
e: abremer@redmundial.com.mx

BELGIUM/NETHERLANDS
Pavan
Thomas Van Theemsche
Meerlaanstraat 73
9860 Balegem (Oostrezele)
Belgium
t: +32 (0) 9 221 85 94
e: pavan@pandora.be

DENMARK
Fancy Knit
Hovedvejen 71, 8586 Oerum
Djurs
Ramten, Denmark
t: +45 59 46 21 89
e: roenneburg@mail.dk

FINLAND
Eiran Tukku
Mäkelänkatu 54 B
00510 Helsinki, Finland
t: +358 50 346 0575
e: maria.hellbom@eirantukku.fi
w: www.eirantukku.fi

FRANCE
Laines Plassard
La Filature
71800 Varennes-sous-Dun
France
t: +33 (0) 3 8528 2828
w: www.laines-plassard.com

GERMANY/AUSTRIA/SWITZERLAND/LUXEMBOURG
Designer Yarns (Deutschland) GmbH
Welserstraße 10g
D-51149 Köln, Germany
t: +49 (0) 2203 1021910
e: info@designeryarns.de
w: www.designeryarns.de

ICELAND
Storkurinn ehf
Laugavegi 59
101 Reykjavík, Iceland
t: +354 551 8258
e: storkurinn@simnet.is

SPAIN
Oyambre Needlework SL
Balmes, 200 At. 4
08006 Barcelona, Spain
t: +34 (0) 93 487 26 72
e: info@oyambreonline.com

SWEDEN
Nysta garn och textil
Hogasvagen 20
S-131 47 Nacka, Sweden
t: +46 (0) 8 612 0330
e: nina@nysta.se
w: www.nysta.se

RUSSIA
Golden Fleece
Soloviyny proezd 16
117593 Moscow, Russia
t: +8 (903) 000 1967
e: natalya@rukodelie.ru
w: www.rukodelie.ru

POLAND
Art-Bijou os
Krakowiakow 5/31
31-962 Krakow, Poland
e: kontakt@artbijou.com

AUSTRALIA/NEW ZEALAND
Prestige Yarns Pty Ltd
PO Box 39, Bulli
NSW 2516, Australia
t: +61 (0) 2 4285 6669
e: info@prestigeyarns.com
w: www.prestigeyarns.com

HONG KONG
East Unity Company Ltd
Unit B2
7/F Block B
Kailey Industrial Centre
12 Fung Yip Street
Chan Wan
t: (852) 2869 7110
e: eastunity@yahoo.com.hk

TAIWAN
U-Knit
1F, 199-1 Sec
Zhong Xiao East Road
Taipei, Taiwan
t: +886 2 27527557
e: shuindigo@hotmail.com

THAILAND
Needle World Co Ltd
Pradit Manoontham Road,
Bangkok 10310
t: 662 933 9167
e: needle-world.coltd@google-mail.com

BRAZIL
Quatro Estacoes Com
Las Linhas e Acessorios Ltda
Av. Das Nacoes Unidas
12551-9 Andar
Cep 04578-000 Sao Paulo
Brazil
t: +55 11 3443 7736
e: cristina@4estacoeslas.com.br

For more information on my other books and yarns, please visit www.debbieblissonline.com

Acknowledgements

This book wouldn't have been possible without the generous collaboration of the following:

Rosy Tucker, who – as I mentioned in my introduction – played such as important part in producing so many of the projects in this book.

Penny Hill, for her essential pattern compiling and organising the knitters.

Jane O'Shea, Lisa Pendreigh and Katherine Case at Quadrille Publishing for being such a wonderful team to work with.

Mia Pejcinovic for the perfect styling and overall look.

Penny Wincer for the beautiful photography.

The knitters, for the huge effort they put into creating perfect knits under deadline pressure: Cynthia Brent, Barbara Clapham, Pat Church, Jacqui Dunt, Shirley Kennet, Maisie Lawrence and Frances Wallace.

My fantastic agent, Heather Jeeves.

The distributors, agents, retailers and knitters who support all my books and yarns with such enthusiasm and, once again, make what I do possible.

Editorial Director Jane O'Shea
Creative Director Helen Lewis
Project Editor Lisa Pendreigh
Designer Katherine Case
Photographer Penny Wincer
Stylist Mia Pejcinovic
Pattern Illustrator Bridget Bodoano
Production Director Vincent Smith
Production Controller Ruth Deary

First published in 2010 by
Quadrille Publishing Limited
Alhambra House
27–31 Charing Cross Road
London WC2H 0LS
www.quadrille.co.uk

Reprinted in 2010
10 9 8 7 6 5 4 3 2

British Library Cataloguing-in-Publication Data
A catalogue record for this book is available from the British Library.

ISBN 978 184400 842 1

Printed in China.